6/19/19

Thanks!

The Q-Factor

The Road to Excellence in Sales and Management

by Frank M. Munson

First published in the United
States of America by:
HSR Publishing Division
of the HSR Group
PO Box 50302
Columbia, SC 29250
1-888-633-5400

Printed and Designed
by Mac Kohn Printing, Inc.
Columbia, SC
2nd Printing

Cover Photo by H. Gordon Humphries
Columbia, SC

Library of Congress Catalog Card Number:
97-74260

ISBN 1-891156-00-4

Dedication

For Betty, my wife of 44 years, whom I've loved and always will.

To my family for all they have meant to me.

To my mother and four sisters who taught me to love.

To Sherry Poole who represents all the caring people that I've worked with who inspired me.

A portion of the royalties from the sales of this book will go to a homeless foundation.

Acknowledgements

So many people have encouraged me to write this book that if I attempted to list them all by name, I might leave someone out. I have truly had a career of learning. Salespeople, managers, friends, and family have influenced me and contributed to my career. I am grateful to each of them.

My editor, Robert Moss, Ph. D., from the University of South Carolina, was a lot of help. Claudia Etheridge, who assisted with the editing, was one of those who encouraged me to complete the book. My publisher was a constant source of encouragement for me to tell my story. Edith Sheets was very helpful with the editing/proofreading. I am also grateful to Walter Kohn, Marlena Crovatt-Bagwell and the creative staff of Mac Kohn Printing for assisting me in the design and printing of *The Q-Factor*.

I am indebted to so many people for inspiration. A desire to contribute to my profession by sharing with other salespeople and managers was always a part of my vision, and like any good compass, it kept me going. Thank you all, very much.

Contents

Preface 2

Foreword 3

Introduction 5

Part One

Searching for Something New 8
  A. New Challenges for the Sunshine Division 9
  B. The Dynamics of Total Quality Management 10
  C. New Ideas for Sales Divisions 12

Part Two

The First Step: Personal Commitment and the Renewal of Spirit . . 15
  A. Personal Vision and Long-term Goals 15
  B. A New Attitude Toward Work and Your Career 19
  C. Risk Taking and Embracing Change 20
  D. Creativity 22
  E. Building Compassionate, Supportive Relationships 24
  F. Renewing and Nurturing the Spirit 27

Part Three

Transforming the Workplace 30
  A. Leadership, Risk Taking, and Celebration 30
  B. A New View of the Customer 33
  C. Customer Guides for Strategic Planning 39
  D. An Illustration of Effective Customer Focus 42
  E. Teamwork 44
  F. Developing A Vision for the Group 49
  G. Breaking Through Limitations 52
  H. Acting on the Vision 54
  I. The Sunshine Division's 10-Point Plan 55
  J. Focusing on Strengths 56
  K. Shifting the Paradigm 57
  L. Shifting Individuals' Paradigms 61

Part Four

Processes and Process Variation 63
   A. Becoming Process-Oriented 63
   B. The FOCUS Process Improvement Strategy. 66

Part Five

The Q-Factor In Action 80
   A. The Payoff 83
   B. Spread of the Q-Factor 85

Part Six

Instilling Trust 86
   A. Trust-Building Actions. 87
   B. Open-Communication Actions 88

Part Seven

Rules of the Road for the Sales Professional 91

Part Eight

Rules of the Road for the Sales Manager 110

Part Nine

About the Author. 152
   A. My first Job in Management. 153
   B. To the Home Office 154
   C. Regional Sales Manager 155
   D. Full Circle 159
   E. Toward a New Way of Managing. 161

Bibliography and Suggested Reading 165

The Q-Factor

The Road to Excellence
in Sales and Management

Preface

Adopt and adapt is the key phrase for this volume. It is modular and designed for random access, so treat it like a CD ROM. No need to begin at the beginning. Everything here is in the most useful form I could employ. Just rely on the Table of Contents and access the information you want in any order you choose.

Part One discusses the need for a new way to manage. Part Two talks about transforming yourself, while Part Three talks about bringing change to the workplace. Parts Four and Five go deeper into the subject, while I tried to boil everything I know down into the straightforward rules of "do's" and "don'ts" that you can find in Parts Seven and Eight. There's one set of rules for salespeople and another for managers, but it wouldn't hurt to read them both. Regardless of your current job title, you probably have already worn, or will one day accept, the other one. If you want to, you can go to "About the Author" to hear about the learning experiences that contributed to the philosophy I call "The Q-Factor."

The salesperson's world has changed and so has that of the manager. No matter how much I might enjoy strolling with you through a traditional discourse on my pet theories of salesmanship and management, I don't have the time and neither do you. So take what you need in the order that you need it, always remembering that the key to success in using any technique is to adopt what is useful and adapt it to your particular circumstance. Be my guest: Find what you need, then adopt and adapt.

Foreword

I have some unsolicited advice for you before you read the first word of this powerful manuscript... turn to page 152 and become familiar with Frank Munson.

Read between the lines as you review his impressive career. Think about some of the decisions he has made. Get a feel for the almost countless times Frank has been recognized for his ability to identify and deliver bottom-line results. Become familiar with the blended passion with which Frank found a way to equitably distribute between the profession he mastered and the family he cherished.

I think you'll find that Frank is a man who truly epitomizes the overused phrase "sales professional." In addition to meeting quotas and helping to build a business, Frank had fun...and he made sure those around him did as well.

Customers liked and respected Frank. Employees developed an enviable sense of loyalty for him. Top management consistently solicited his advice on business strategy. In short, Frank Munson has forgotten more than most of us will ever know about the process of successfully influencing other people.

Fortunately for us, Frank has taken the time to document the keys to his success. You have undoubtedly read about vision, goal-setting, risk taking, and change management before. Frank's take on those and other topics combines a concise, theoretical review with a field-tested, applications-based orientation. In other words, if you are actually interested in how to establish a personal vision, set goals, take risks, or manage change...read Parts 2 and 3 of this book!

Now, just for the sake of example, let's say you don't have a significant amount of spare time to invest in "development reading." In his aptly-named chapters on "Rules of the Road" for salespeople and sales managers, Frank condenses a lifetime of experience into a series of thought-provoking bullet points.

In essence, the "Rules of the Road" are quick reference lists you can review before heading out into the field each day. These are lists of things to do...or in some cases, things to avoid...that will assist you in your efforts to sell and/or manage in an increasingly complex environment. By the way, if you're expecting these bullet points to contain tactically-based techniques that require limited effort and ensure overnight success, you will surely be disappointed. Frank's advice can best be described as "focused fuel for introspection."

It is my opinion that if you honestly review Frank Munson's words of time-tested wisdom...and compare his advice to the manner in which you currently sell to your customers and/or manage your salespeople...at a minimum, you are sure to gain valuable personal insight!

–Roger Dow
VP & General Sales Manager
for Marriott Lodging

INTRODUCTION

A Time for Change

The requirements of management today are suddenly very different, and as managers we must meet the needs of a new environment. The old authoritative style of management by objectives—goal setting with praises and reprimands—no longer works so well. We are learning that we need a better way.

Life in the Information Age means that computers can organize and make available more and more hard data for people to base business decisions on. These decisions, however, frequently fail to inspire managers and workers with the commitment and desire to implement that is necessary to achieve goals. In our haste to design better corporations, we have taken very little time to explore and address the human and emotional needs generated by those decisions. We have overlooked the necessity for establishing compassion, caring, understanding, higher responsibility and accountability as essential elements of effective management. Although we want to hold workers accountable for results, we have expressed a lack of trust in their skills and commitment by overdirecting their activities.

In an era when people are more aware of their emotional needs, the same old managerial styles no longer work. We must learn to manage our salespeople and service our customers with compassion, with heart, and with a sincere degree of caring. We must provide security and self-fulfillment in the workplace, along with the abundance of challenge that we hand out.

We have not fully addressed our customers' needs. We've been so busy trying to meet our own needs and goals that we've mostly given lip service to the needs and goals of our customers. We have neglected to learn about the customers' feelings and perceptions, and we've shown too little respect for their suggestions regarding our products and services. Most of all, we have forgotten that the road to success requires well-tended and mutually-beneficial relationships between ourselves and all the people we work with...and that means the customers we serve, as well as the leaders of our organizations, our peers, our suppliers, and even the competition.

We must build a workplace that is better than the one we have now. The challenges of the future business world demand it. In the absence of traditional work structures, we need to create work environments that are safe and secure, that are supportive, and that encourage learning. When we bring compassion and accountability to our business relationships, we create an environment in which people can step out of their comfort zone to take risks, to fail, to grow, and to learn. People want to feel and believe that you care about them as well as business. Financial numbers are important, but in order to guarantee them, we must look beyond short-term results and toward the longer-range benefits of a supportive workplace.

Along with building new relationships, it is essential that we adopt new, effective ways of doing business every day. Companies have gotten so caught up in not taking risks that they have become stagnant in their methods and techniques. In order to change that, we need only recognize and stay receptive to the provocative new ways of thinking about business that are available to us.

What follows is a compilation and discussion of outstanding techniques that have been tremendously effective during my own career as a salesman and as the leader of a highly successful sales division. Derived partially from the ideas of Dr. W. Edwards Deming and others, they form a comprehensive approach to quality-based management—a process by which a sales organization can redefine itself and make itself more responsive to today's changing marketplace. Because a concern for quality in all aspects of our work as managers is the key factor in this process, I call this process *The Q-Factor*.

This book is written for salespeople and sales managers. *The Q-Factor* is intended to help you evaluate where you are now, determine what opportunities exist for you in the future, and help you find the direction for your personal and professional journey. Obviously, since each person and each company is different, any new program must be tailored to suit that company's structure and needs. By following these guidelines and examples, however, you will have the basic ideas and strategies for bringing *The Q-Factor* into your career, your workgroup and your company.

1

PART ONE

Searching for Something New

After progressing rapidly through the ranks of a major corporation—from salesman to sales trainer to division manager, to department head in the home office, to regional manager—I had decided to return to my first love, the position of division sales manager in my own hometown. I came back to the Sunshine Division determined to apply all that I had learned about sales and management.

Working with some great salespeople had taught me a lot, and I had taken advantage of every management course that had come my way. Management techniques I had observed in the home office added to my repertoire, and I was sure that I knew exactly what to do to help bring success and respect to the Sunshine Division.

And everything worked...for quite some time. Things were going great for the Sunshine Division. Business was excellent, the salespeople were happy, and we were winning sales awards. But subtle changes were taking place in our markets. Competitors were adding more and more salespeople. Customers were becoming more difficult to see. Prices and cost-control were becoming the main topics of concern. Our major product had achieved the number-one position in market share, but sixteen large competitors were trying to break into the business. When you're on top, everyone else starts gunning for you. Competition was greatly increasing, and our cost of doing business was rising. In other words, the world changed.

New Challenges for the Sunshine Division

People no longer expect, as their parents did, to follow a predictable career track throughout their working lives. Employees are buffeted by conditions that they have never dealt with before, frightening situations such as:

- periodic recessions
- downsizing of companies, organizations, and government
- cutbacks in workforce
- reduction in the number of middle managers
- a decline in the job market for recent college graduates
- a trend of decreasing productivity for U.S. workers

Is it any wonder that people in the workplace increasingly seek pride and self-fulfillment from sources other than their jobs and careers? Even when they are not aware of exactly what is lacking in their vocations, people know that something is gone. But try as they may, through leisure-time activities, hobbies, sidelines, volunteer work, and community service, they cannot find replacements for what they are missing in their jobs. People cannot make up elsewhere for something that is absent all day long in their work life.

Our methods had worked well in the past, but something different was going to be needed to meet the new challenges of this changing market. Having a top-performing product is great for bottom-line sales, but it can pose a danger for the future because you don't spend enough time, energy, and money to continue your success, prepare for changes in business, and improve results even more. We in the Sunshine

Division realized that we needed to reassess what we were doing, so according to a process which I'll describe later, we met, discussed the situation, and together decided to change.

As we listed them at the time, these were some of our reasons for changing:

- To increase productivity even more
- To reduce costs
- To maximize the potential of people, products, policies, and performance
- To handle the competition's onslaught
- To cope with the demands for a better price
- To stay in business—and on top of the business

To meet these goals, I looked both to what I had learned in the past and to new ideas that might be applied to the Sunshine Division. Business thinkers such as W. Edwards Deming (whose philosophy of Total Quality Management is receiving greater and greater credence) and others have given us the clues to improving productivity and moving successfully into a more competitive global society, which we began to explore thoroughly. Elements of what became the Q-Factor were beginning to emerge; one of them coming, not from management philosophy, but from the world of manufacturing.

The Dynamics of Total Quality Management

From the moment I first learned about Total Quality Management (T.Q.M.), I became an evangelical student. Newspaper articles about state agencies using T.Q.M. first stimulated my interest, then I began hearing that leading companies such as Milliken, the giant, privately-held textile company, had embraced the philosophy. Many hospitals, even entire communities, were setting up excellence programs based on T.Q.M. principles.

The man behind T.Q.M. is W. Edwards Deming. As a business consultant, he learned early that statistical analysis and product quality offered advantages in a competitive market, and he helped install statistical quality control (S.Q.C.) in many U.S. factories. In the post-WWII economic boom, however, American industry faced no real competition, and Dr. Deming was unable to earn widespread recognition in our country. Businesses were focused primarily on quantity: they were too busy churning out products to be very concerned about quality.

Deming's ideas found their first audience when General Douglas MacArthur asked him to help the Japanese rebuild their war-shattered industries. Deming became deeply involved with the presidents of Japan's leading companies and convinced them that they could compete in the worldwide market by producing quality goods. Dr. Deming also taught the Japanese the importance of making the customer part of the production process. They were successful, and in no time at all the world's perception of products made in Japan changed from seeing them as cheap and shoddy to considering them to be of world-class quality.

In 1980, NBC televised a documentary entitled, "If Japan Can—Why Can't We?" The program told the story of how Dr. Deming's philosophy had revolutionized Japanese industry. This exposure opened doors for him at major American industries, and he began conducting seminars at Georgetown University in Washington, D.C. Since then, his influence has continued to grow.

The basis of Dr. Deming's philosophy is embodied in his 14-Point Plan for the Transformation of Management, which you can and should check out in his book, *Out of the Crisis.*

The U.S. quality movement took root with manufacturing companies such as Ford, General Motors, Chrysler, I.B.M., Digital Equipment, Hewlett-Packard, Proctor & Gamble, Motorola, Xerox, Eastman Kodak, Polaroid, Texas Instruments, and Milliken & Company. The ideas then spread to the health-care profession. In October 1989, The Health Care Forum launched its first Quality Improvement Network (QIN) as a forum for information exchange on each organization's quality program. Health Care leaders are now at the forefront of the quality-improvement movement. T.Q.M. is now making inroads into a wide variety of companies and even noncommercial enterprises such as the administration of public schools.

New Ideas for Sales Divisions

Despite the popularity of the T.Q.M. movement, its methods have been slow to come to the field of sales. Many people feel that T.Q.M. does not apply to salespeople, and it has been documented how infrequently and slowly efforts for quality improvement are adapted by sales forces. There are several reasons for this sluggishness:

- The customer has rarely been put in the most important position. We say that our customers are the most important link in our supply chain, but we measure our success in terms of numbers: numbers of sales, numbers of calls, numbers of presentations. All these are important, but they emphasize quantity over quality. They do not help us meet or exceed customers' expectations and fulfill their wants and needs.
- Obviously, there will always be bottom-line requirements for numbers and figures, and we don't know whether we can have a customer-driven quality program and still meet these requirements.
- Perhaps most important, we don't know what we can do to initiate a quality-improvement program without extensive training programs that would keep salespeople out of the field for too long.

If I achieve nothing more in this book than answering these concerns, my efforts will be worthwhile.

We can and must put the customer first. Salespeople are the best-qualified to implement a quality-improvement program because they are the ones in direct contact with the customer. The bottom line is where the results will be, but the real numbers—that is, profits—will increase as the sales force is allowed to satisfy customers first and eliminate the cost involved with unnecessary work and nonproductive activities.

It will take more than a few changes. It will require abandoning long-held practices of management that are now outdated and inefficient. We have traditionally trained and rewarded salespeople to be:

- detail, not process-oriented
- proficient in product knowledge, but not in customer knowledge
- concerned with short-term rather than long-term goals
- responsive to quotas set in the home office instead of goals they established in consultation with management
- focused on calls and presentations instead of satisfying customers

This orientation makes it very difficult to move toward quality improvement. If we are going in this direction, sales training and strategies must change. We must increase the emphasis on simulations that prepare salespeople to respond quickly and effectively to customer requests, needs, opportunities, and problems. We must teach our salespeople to understand customer needs so they can truly help their customers become more efficient and effective. Salespeople can be trained to recognize and respond quickly to selling situations in creative, relevant ways and not to simply recite product features and benefits.

Continuous improvement requires continuous innovation. Companies that will excel today and tomorrow can't think about the way they did it yesterday. They must redesign their organization to support and focus on the customer, the local market, creativity, innovation, flexibility, and Total Quality Management. And their managers must be ready.

The combination of new skills, individualized professional expertise, and a profound commitment to quality required of the manager today is so unusual that we can think of it as a whole new factor for success, one I think of as the "Q-Factor." Let me share with you how an amalgamation of successful management techniques that I call the "Q-Factor" were applied in one division of a major corporation. They may help you evolve your own personalized—and hugely successful—version of the *"Q-Factor."*

2

PART TWO

Personal Commitment and the Renewal of Spirit

The first step on the road to the Q-Factor begins within ourselves. If you stop and think about it, this only makes sense. Unfortunately, with all the new business ideas floating around out there—the flavors of the month, if you will—we too often fall into the trap of believing that real change in our workplace can come just by making a few alterations in the way we conduct business. Implement a new data-tracking system here, initiate a new rewards program there—and like that we've transformed our sales division, right?

Wrong. Making specific changes in the workplace is important, but they won't be very effective unless more basic changes are made to prepare for them. Putting new siding on a house won't be any use if the foundation is crumbling. Salespeople and sales managers who are getting ready to begin a program of change must first ask themselves, "What do I need to do to personally prepare myself for the journey to come? How can I make changes within myself that will make possible the changes I want to make within my company?" This is the first step.

Personal Vision and Long-Term Goals

Throughout this book, you will see a pattern in our approach to making changes within ourselves, our work group, and our company. First we'll look to the long-term future, toward overall, general goals. Then we'll move back to the underlying attitudes and ideas that control how we live and react in the present. Finally, we'll look at specific steps that can be made to implement change.

Begin then with your personal vision of who you are and what you want to be. And what, after all, is a vision? It involves goals, plans, and objectives, but it's more than just those things. Many of us have been so busy setting and meeting goals and objectives that we have forgotten visions and dreams. A vision is broader, more noble, and—most important—more motivating than goals and objectives. It is a picture of ourselves in the future we want to inhabit. The clearer this picture is, the easier it will be to make the daily choices and decisions that will get us where we want to go. A vision will move us to set goals and objectives with checkpoints, activities, relationships, and time frames.

A friend of mine who teaches college freshmen wanted to get his students thinking about the value of a college education and what they hoped to achieve during their four years on campus. To get the ball rolling, he had the students ask themselves, among other things, "Where do you envision yourself ten years from now? Where do you think you'll live? What do you think you will be doing? What kind of person do you think you'll be?" A few of the students gave imaginative, interesting responses, such as "I hope to be living abroad and photographing nature and wild animals for a living." But, the vast majority of the responses—to the teacher's surprise—were dull and routine: "I hope to be married, have a family and a nice home, and a good job."

There's nothing wrong with wanting these things. After all, who wouldn't want them? But it was troubling that so few of the students had given specific thought to their futures. The only answers they could come up with about their dreams were of the same general vagueness that most people share. They had no individual, personal vision to guide them. These students were eighteen years old, still inexperienced and, hopefully, filled with the rather naive idealism of youth. If their dreams were so dull at that early age, how much duller would they be once the students got out in the working world and experienced a little disillusionment?

Fortunately, it is never too late to sit down and formulate a personal vision. The details of the job or the home or the possessions you will have ten, twenty, thirty, or more years down the road are not that significant. The important thing is your own vision of yourself, who you want to be. You need to be able to close your eyes and have a clear mental picture of what the future will look like and feel like. How will you look? How will others perceive you? Imagine all the details, as if you were a third-person observer or a hidden movie camera. Where will you be? What will the surrounding backdrop look like? How will you sound? What gestures will you make? What will you say and do? What kind of people will be around you? What will they look like and act like?

Imagine yourself in some of the following situations:
- interacting with your family at home—while eating dinner, for example
- enjoying a Saturday afternoon with friends
- relaxing alone in your free time
- making a speech and seeing the audience responding in a positive way
- making a sales call, and seeing your customers satisfied and buying your product
- working with members of your sales team and seeing them reacting positively and doing what you want

Don't try to force the visualization. Let it flow from inside yourself, from your intuition and imagination. Don't try to shape it to fit the picture of how others think your future should be planned.

Take the time to be quiet. We can't listen if we are busy thinking, doing, talking, responding, skipping ahead, and saying what can't be done, and attacking and talking to ourselves when we should be listening:

Listen to your inner thoughts.

Listen to your spirit.

Listen to your intuitions.

Listen to your aspirations.

Listen to your dreams.

More than anything, be sure to listen to your religious faith and personal values. Consider how you want to behave, how you want to treat the people around you. Before you can move ahead you must know the kind of person you want to become in the future.

Once you have that image—a specific, concrete vision of yourself, you can fill in the surrounding details as you go. Think of yourself as a painter who starts with a single image in the middle of a blank canvas. He first makes broad brush strokes, then adds more color and details as he goes along. We will need to add more clarity, color, and form to our personal vision, but we have to have the broad initial image to guide the addition of detail.

We should dream high dreams and have high goals that are related to serving ourselves and others in a wiser, more loving, and more caring manner. Our vision should include the following:

• to serve the most people possible

• to develop our own character

• to utilize our strengths

• to free ourselves from a specific time frame

• to be open to new and additional dreams

• to have some clarity and detail, but to retain some vagueness and ambiguity as well

Having a vision is not like creating goals, which are more like milestones along the way. A vision works like a compass. If we lose direction or stray from the path, consulting our vision will bring us back on track eventually. And the clearer the vision, the quicker the course correction.

Once you have a strong sense of your personal vision—and once you are firmly committed to it—you can move forward and begin setting the goals and objectives and making the inner changes necessary for achieving that vision.

A New Attitude Toward Work and Your Career

Attitude isn't something imposed upon us from the outside. It's a choice. Some people respond to an uncertain business climate by distancing themselves from their jobs and seeking fulfillment in sources outside their work. Their heavy emotional investment may go into hobbies and other leisure-time activities, for example. But isolating our identity and sense of spiritual well-being from our work denies a crucial fact: our jobs are a vital aspect of our lives, and each day we spend an enormous amount of our time at work.

Consider these numbers. There are 168 hours in a week. If you sleep seven hours a night, then that leaves you with 119 hours awake. Assuming you work 40 hours a week (and most people today work far more) and must spend 2 hours each day preparing for and commuting to and from work (again, a very conservative figure,) then 50 hours a week—or almost half the time you are awake—is occupied with your job or job-related activities. Trying to separate personal fulfillment from your work means discarding almost half your life as unfulfilling. And how much of what remains can really provide fulfillment? A certain portion of our nonworking life must be spent on routine necessities such as paying bills, maintaining a home, having the car serviced, and going to the dentist.

For our lives to be full and worthwhile, we must enjoy our work, look forward to it, and draw personal satisfaction from it. This does not mean making work the sole focus of life: becoming so involved in a career that we neglect family and friends is just as bad as viewing our job as nothing more than a source of income. What we need to achieve is a balance between our professional lives and our personal lives. We must adapt ourselves so that even in a business climate of uncertainty and instability we can be comfortable and can excel in our jobs and our careers. Doing so requires that we change the way we think about work and change the way we react to the conditions of the workplace.

Risk Taking and Embracing Change

To adapt ourselves for maximum career fulfillment, we must change the way we personally approach challenges and adversity. The natural human response when stability and the old ways of doing things are threatened is to retreat, to draw back into a defensive position and resist the changes. When our department's budget is being threatened with cuts, we argue as strongly as we can that we need that money and can't operate effectively without it. When facing personnel cuts or restructuring, we may fight to keep the people we have and argue for their value. These reactions are normal, even commendable.

But what do we do when we cannot stop the changes, when the cuts or restructurings are instituted despite our protests? If we were to maintain a defensive position, brooding about change, it would foster a negative climate within our division or work group. After a certain point, clinging to the old ways becomes destructive and prevents the group from functioning and improving within the new circumstances.

Even when the familiar way of doing business is not being threatened, an overreliance on security and the status quo is harmful for job performance. It is all too easy to do just enough to get by. Trying to implement change involves taking risks, and taking risks involves the possibility of failure. Too often, rather than risking failure we stay with the old methods and practices. This is the safe route, but it also cuts off any possibility of advancement. Safety is the most unrewarding goal to work toward. It keeps us from learning new things and gets in the way of our reaching our true potential. We need a new attitude toward taking chances and making changes.

Part of becoming committed to a new personal vision of yourself is consciously pushing yourself to make difficult choices and actively seek change. Begin attempting activities that you are not particularly comfortable with, even those as simple as striking up a conversation with someone you haven't been able to get to know very well, or raising a concern with others in your work group. The more you push the boundaries of comfort, the more you will become able to take risks and make difficult decisions.

An important part of risk taking is personal responsibility. You can't have one without the other. You can expect that some risks will pay off, but you must also expect some to fail. When you take a chance and make a mistake, be accountable for your actions. Admit you made an error, and explain why you under-took the step in the first place. Honesty and accountability is a key. But there is a payoff: even when you make mistakes, you can learn from them. You can grow.

And that's the whole point of risk taking and changing: ulti-mately, they lead to new knowledge and personal growth. Whenever change comes your way, don't ask yourself, "What can I do to cope with this and ride it out?" Ask instead, "What can I do to embrace these challenges, to learn from them, and ultimately improve myself and advance my personal vision?"

The business world today offers us a host of challenges that, at times, seem to bear down and smother us. If we look those challenges in the eye and see them as an opportunity for growth, learning, and improvement, we will begin changing the way we view our jobs and the purpose of our work.

Creativity

Webster defines "create" as, 1. to cause to come into existence; make, originate. 2. to cause; produce; bring about. These definitions suggest that creative thoughts have to be original, brand new, and never before tried. How many times have you heard people say, when they meet a person with a talent for writing or art, "I really envy you. I wish I were creative myself." Our standard notions of creativity are very restrictive, breaking the world up into a small number of creative people and a vast majority of uncreative people.

Is this division really accurate, though? Certainly, few of us are ever going to try our hand at writing a novel, painting a portrait, or creating a sculpture. But this doesn't mean that we cannot be creative. Creativity is not so much a talent as a way of thinking, which is something that can be learned and expanded. It involves the willingness to experiment and make changes, a confidence in one's own skills and capabilities, and the ability to adapt useful ideas to your own circumstances.

Let's look a little closer at that last dictionary definition of creativity. If we accepted it literally, then we would believe that we couldn't be creative unless we were doing things and thinking thoughts that no one has ever come up with before. But there is no writer, painter, or any other artist who doesn't have models and masters from whom they have learned their techniques and received inspiration. The early work of virtually every great novelist and poet is highly imitative of the writers they admire. Only as they mature and develop do they begin to develop their own style and discover their own individual material. Some forms of art, in fact, such as the collage and digitally-sampled music, involve no original material at all. The individuality of the work—indeed, the creativity—exists solely in the way in which the borrowed material is arranged and adapted.

Creativity, then, is not in the ideas and techniques we use but rather in how we use them. Anyone can learn to be creative. We must simply look for new ideas and different ways of doing things while always taking into consideration how we can adapt those ideas for our own use. Too often when we are searching for new ways of doing things, we are looking for "recipes" that we can follow step by step without having to modify any details. That's far easier than coming up with our own plan, but it has its dangers. Consider, for example, the countless fad diets that are printed in magazines each week. If you want to lose weight, they claim, all you have to do is follow this simple step-by-step plan. It all sounds so easy, but these diets never really seem to work. How could they? Everyone's body is different, and one person's schedule and habits are different from another's. A single diet can't work for everyone.

The same can be said for plans and methods for improving business. Every week, new books are published that are loaded down with charts, graphs, plans, and techniques. No business person could ever hope to implement all the plans; very few of us could fully implement any individual plan. Companies vary too much. Problems are often specific to particular industries or markets. Even the personalities and abilities of those we work with shape what we can do within our individual companies.

This is by no means to say that these books and plans are without merit. Oftentimes they are filled with wonderful ideas, even though their schemes can't work for us as a whole. We need to approach these resources with creativity, considering what the authors have to say and analyzing the ideas they are laying out. After asking ourselves which of the ideas are relevant for our personal and professional situation, we can adopt the material we find useful, and adapt it to our own needs.

(That goes, of course, for the ideas contained in this book as well. Adopt and adapt as you see fit.)

In order to implement change, we must be receptive to new ideas. We must seek them out, wrestle with them, and decide which ones are most valuable. Then, we must be creative and thoughtful in applying them to our own divisions and work groups. Be creative and bring creativity to your job, career, and personal life.

Building Compassionate, Supportive Relationships

Thus far in this chapter we have been talking about making individual changes, changes in how we think about ourselves and our jobs. Now it is time to move beyond the personal level to think about how we interact with the people around us.

The traditional business climate encouraged us to view other people as either competitors that we must outdo or as tools we can use to advance our own ends. This can be called a self-oriented stance. When a company is under the threat of layoffs and downsizing, this stance becomes even more pronounced. We can feel we are fighting for our jobs and see the people around us as a threat to our careers.

But is the self-oriented stance the best way? Is it the right way? The suspicion and infighting that tough times bring is a human response, but it is often counterproductive. By trying to make themselves look good (and their peers look bad), self-oriented people cut off channels of support, hinder effective operation, and stifle improvement. In the effort to improve their own performance, they actually hurt it.

What we need in today's sales world is to move toward an outward-oriented stance, where the needs and concerns of other people are given top priority. In a moral and ethical sense, it is the right thing to do. In a bottom-line business sense, it is a useful, effective way to maximize our own potential and the potential of our division and work group. We will discuss the more specific business elements of this philosophy in upcoming chapters, but for now let's consider how we can bring an outward-oriented stance to our everyday lives.

The first step is to listen, to take the time to hear what the people around us have to say. We must keep our own personal vision and goals in mind, but at the same time we need to be able to appreciate and address what other people need and want. It's far more realistic to see ourselves not as individuals on solitary journeys but as partners with others on a similar path. Take the time to consider the people around you, to learn who they are and what they are doing. This concern must be genuine, not a sham intended to manipulate and influence other people. Our relationships must begin sincerely, one-to-one, on a person-to-person basis. The payoffs will be enormous.

Make a determined effort to improve your listening skills. Concentrate on making eye contact and focus on the other person while he or she is speaking. Listen with your whole body. Ask questions and block out distractions. Most importantly, strive not to just hear what the other person is saying but to truly understand it. It is easy enough to make a person believe that you are listening and understanding, but it is harder to develop a true connection and concern. How many times do we nod our heads and make eye contact but allow the other person's words to go in one ear and out the other? Many times in a conversation we are so busy thinking about what we will say next that we do not really understand what the other person is saying. Good listening involves genuine concern and understanding. When we listen well, we begin to learn, and we begin to appreciate the value of the people around us.

Teach yourself to see the good in other people. We all know that no one is perfect, so we should expect to find flaws and weaknesses in those we deal with on a daily basis. It is tempting to identify these weaknesses and to try to correct them—

particularly if we are in a position of leadership or authority.
We should be aware of and concerned with the limitations of
our coworkers, but that cannot be the only thing we think
about. It is far more important to identify their strengths and
attempt to nurture those strengths. Doing so will often resolve
weaknesses and limitations.

Consider this real-life example of a trainer for a large corporation who conducts three-day seminars for new hires to teach
them the company ropes. Because the trainees were coming
into entry-level positions, most of them were relatively young,
some fresh out of college. One trainee, however, was an older
woman who had been in business for more than a decade, even
owning her own company for a while. Throughout the first
day's session she seemed bored and, as the class went on,
became more and more ill-mannered, as if she were resentful of
having to be there. Her inattention became obvious, she
fidgeted constantly, and soon she was making sarcastic
comments under her breath about the material being covered.

The training leader knew that she had a problem on her
hands. The older trainee's attitude seemed to be infectious,
making the other members of the seminar restless and uneasy.
By the end of the first day the leader knew she would have to
have a talk with the woman about her conduct and attitude—
and even considered asking her not to return for the rest of the
sessions. The new trainee seemed to have an attitude problem,
a personality not well suited for the company. It was a serious
weakness and limitation, and the trainer knew she had to either
remedy the situation or let the trainee go.

That evening, however, the members of the seminar all went
out to dinner. The training leader ended up sitting next to the
woman with whom she'd had so many problems earlier in the
day. As they ate they began talking; the trainer began to understand the woman more. She had recently moved back to the
East Coast to be near family and friends and found it difficult

to find a new job. She was very conscious of being the oldest one in the group, felt insecure about starting over at an entry level position, and was afraid the others in the seminar looked down on her for that.

The trainer began to see that these problems were linked to some valuable strengths. The trainee had years of experience in customer relations—more, in fact, than the trainer herself. She knew ways of dealing with problem customers and ensuring satisfaction that could—and should—be shared with the others in the group. The leader decided to capitalize on these strengths. She encouraged the older trainee to speak up during the sessions, to share her thoughts on the things with which she was experienced. As a result, the woman began to feel more at ease in the group, behaving as if she were part of it and there for a purpose. Her weaknesses—her insecurity and disruptive attitude—were alleviated by understanding and nurturing her strengths.

Getting outside ourselves and learning to understand and appreciate the people around us is an essential part of building a healthy climate within our companies, divisions, and work groups. When we do so, we begin to develop a feeling of partnership, of working together toward common goals. Fostering these types of compassionate, supportive relationships is a key element of providing a feeling of stability and security in the modern workplace.

Renewing and Nurturing the Spirit

How's your spirit? "Spirit" is a rather abstract term, but it involves our energy, our enthusiasm, our determination, our desire, and our commitment. It is what moves our real selves. It inspires us to work as hard as we possibly can. It gives us a sense of purpose and fulfillment in our jobs. It is what makes success possible. And if you're not careful, it can be stressed by the concerns of the modern environment.

Just consider the impact of factors such as:

Personal and Family Problems
- both husband and wife working, with little time for relaxation
- money problems
- concerns about the cost of a college education for children
- concerns about elderly parents
- divorce
- health problems and concerns about what we eat, drink, and weigh

Social Considerations
- concern over the survival of Social Security and Medicare
- unrealistic expectations
- violence and crime

Information and Technological Pressures
- information overload: too much to take in and interpret properly
- because it's possible, the pressure to work continually: in the car, home, office, wherever you are
- equipment becoming outdated before you learn how to use it
- new equipment causing distraction, frustration, and down-time from the real job
- increased statistic-gathering techniques leading to numbers overkill

Impersonal Workplace
- larger companies where we know fewer coworkers personally
- more travel
- concern over replacement by temporary or out-sourced workers
- less face-to-face contact because of e-mail, teleconferencing, and fax machines

Virtually everyone in sales today is feeling the strain of these factors. Is there any question in your mind that our own spirit and that of the people around us needs attention and nurturing?

Once you have identified and acknowledged the conditions threatening your spirit and that of the people around you, it is time to begin renewing that spirit, to bring energy, meaning, and purpose back to yourself and your fellow workers.

As you read the following chapters, always remember to approach the ideas you find with thought and creativity. Ponder how they might apply to you and how you might adapt them for your own work situation. Always remember your vision and try to use these ideas to achieve it. Modifying our personal outlook and behavior is the first step in achieving the Q-Factor.

3

PART THREE

Transforming The Workplace

Leadership, Risk Taking, and Celebration

The great emphasis placed on supervision in today's business world causes several problems. Perhaps most harmful is that oversupervision limits the potential of the salespeople by not recognizing how much they have to offer to the productivity of the overall organization. This potential needs to be maximized, not restricted. Under the standard system, a large percentage of salespeople are doing only enough to get by in their jobs. They are being over-managed and underled.

We have too many managers and supervisors today who are primarily interested in finding out what salespeople are *not* doing, what they *do not* know, and what they need to improve. This attitude is often caused by the managers' misperception of their role within the company. They see themselves primarily as helping the salespeople improve their performance; therefore, the managers believe that in order to be useful, they must find something that the salespeople need to improve: sales results, knowledge, activities, or skills.

Too often, managers or supervisors can teach only the rules and regulations that are outlined in their procedure manuals. They can't teach anything further because the students have not shown up. These students—the salespeople—do not want to learn; doing so is an admission that they lack something, something that will be pointed out by the manager. Or, they don't want to learn because they are busy keeping up a front and covering up their needs. They don't want these needs to be discovered because they will then be punished with low-performance appraisals or with more so-called training. Add to this situation the anxiety caused by the climate of downsizing and the increase in competition—both from other companies and within the salespeople's own company—and the result is heightened feelings of insecurity.

The way to overcome this insecurity is by replacing mere *management* with effective *leadership.* There are several things you can do to reach the position of leadership:

1. **Make a firm decision that you want to move from the role of manager/supervisor to that of a manager/ leader.**

2. **Look for the good that is within all of us:** yourself, salespeople, customers, and everyone you come into contact with each day. Within every problem or challenge there is a potential for learning. Begin looking for that potential.

3. **Create a culture or environment that is supportive of learning, encourages risk taking, develops empowerment, and does not blindly punish failure.** We are bound to fail in some of the goals we set, and we are bound to encounter some problems that we cannot solve. Our sales teams need to feel safe in learning by trial and error. Oftentimes we learn far more from our mistakes than from our successes. Leaders are people who have learned how to "reward failure." In doing so they are encouraging learning and creativity, stepping off the beaten path, and taking control.

4. **Encourage celebration and having fun.** An environment that is supportive of learning and risk taking can be a lot of fun for those who are a part of it. When we have identified problems or weaknesses, we should not feel disappointed or afraid and should not attempt to cover up what we have found. We should instead celebrate our discovery: it has taught us something we didn't know before and given us a sense of direction that we might not have found otherwise. When we are learning we are able to share with others. This learning needs to be celebrated in the groups we belong to. The more fun and celebration you can put into a work group, the less stress there will be in the environment. Fun and celebration should be a vital part of the recognition and rewards given for progress. It spurs improvement, makes the group more alive, and gives support and encouragement to all the members of the team.

5. **Welcome change.** Anticipate it, embrace it, and encourage it. The easiest path to take is to maintain the current course. It may not be the best course, but we are familiar with it and know its limitations and problems. If we stick with it, we will avoid further troubles: we will also never see further improvement. Searching for a better way to do things brings new risks and unforeseen problems, but it also brings new benefits and unforeseen rewards. A supervisor simply sticks to the tried-and-true way of doing things; a leader looks for new and better ways. To bring leadership to your company, division, or work group, you must be committed to fostering and embracing change.

A New View of the Customer

One of the first changes that needs to be implemented in sales divisions today is to revolutionize the way managers and salespeople view their customers. Management-by-results or management-by-objectives (or whatever you want to call the old philosophy) caused companies to look inward at themselves rather than outward at the world in which the customer operates. Success measurements have been based on meeting numerical goals and lists of objectives, and the customer has been left out of the equation. The importance of providing a product or service that works and that satisfies the customer has gone unrecognized. To change this pattern of management, we must give customer needs and concerns top priority. We must study and constantly improve every work process so that the final product or service meets—or, even better—exceeds our customers' expectations.

The elements of this new attitude toward customers can be broken down in a list of old versus new ideas:

Old	*New*
1. Selling to customers	1. Partnership with customers
2. Quality in numbers	2. Quality determined by customers
3. Quality is quantity	3. Customer satisfaction
4. Assume what the customer needs	4. Learn, anticipate, and fulfill individual customer needs
5. Service only to increase sales	5. Service to add value and build relationships
6. Work against customer agenda	6. Work within customer agenda
7. How to sell to customers	7. How customers buy
8. Customer knowledge	8. Knowledge of the customer's business
9. Information about customer's market or segment	9. Information about individual customer's business
10. Sell to customers	10. Collaborate w/customers

As we make these changes in our approach to customers, our bottom-line numbers will improve. Today's customers are demanding a better price and quality. They are going to start— and in some instances already are—developing lists of "preferred vendors." They are not going to keep doing business with every supplier. W. Edwards Deming recognized this fact and incorporated it into the 4th Point of his 14-Point Plan for Transforming Management:

> *Stop doing business on price tag alone. Instead minimize total cost. Move toward a long-term relationship of loyalty and trust.*

Will we be on the list of "preferred vendors?" Will we be the one supplier that our customers most want to do business with? That is the challenge facing salespeople and managers today. And, like every challenge or crisis, it offers opportunities for the salespeople, managers, and companies to make a new commitment to serving the customer better.

When we change our attitude or thinking, our behavior will naturally change as well. One of the first things that will happen is that we will make more quality sales calls. Think about a friend of yours—a real friend. Isn't your behavior toward him or her different from your behavior toward mere acquaintances? And does the number of real friends you have make any difference in your behavior to one of them? You are geared toward each friend as an individual when you are with them. You're less judgmental, and you listen more. You care for them without expectations. They receive your attention, you share and learn from each other, and you trust and enjoy each other.

We spend a lot of time with our customers. Is there any reason why we shouldn't treat them as well as we do our friends? Such an approach will not only improve bottom-line sales figures but also bring more pride and enjoyment to our work and increase our confidence for the future.

We must make individual customers our center of interest and activity. We need a well-defined image of each customer and knowledge of what is distinctive about her or him. Customer focus means going the extra mile to ensure that we have exhausted every possible way of satisfying the people we sell to. This effort should cover everything from demonstrating the highest degree of professionalism when we deal with customers on the phone to our response to customers' requests and an ability to customize unique packages of products and services tailor-made to our customers' needs. Here's just a partial list of the elements of customer focus:

Elements of Customer Focus
- Building customer confidence
- Taking ownership when solving problems
- Making and meeting commitments to customers
- Responding to customers in a timely, accurate fashion
- Seeking out and responding to customer suggestions
- Identifying and understanding customers and their needs
- Establishing productive relationships with customers
- Maintaining relationships with influential-thought leaders
- Assisting customers with their training needs
- Having a clear understanding of the customer's business
- Taking proactive steps toward helping customers achieve their business needs and critical success factors—the things that companies, divisions, groups, or individuals must do to succeed in their market.

Let's look closer at the last element, helping customers achieve their critical success factors (CSFs). The tendency is for us to ignore these factors and focus solely on our product's qualities and advantages. We want to just take the order and get out of Dodge. Rarely do we stop and consider what our customer is trying to achieve. If we do actually consider this, too often we merely assume that we know what the customer needs and build this assumption around our particular product. It is far better to sit down, discuss the customer's overall needs, and try to see them from his or her perspective.

Suppose we represent a supplier who sells a line of prepared frozen appetizers to independent restaurants. One of our best customers has been Hank's Place, a seafood and steak restaurant in a popular nightlife district. Our standard promotional materials highlight the features of each individual product: attractive appearance, easy preparation, large portions for a relatively low food-cost. During our standard sales call, we sit down with Hank and show him the promotional materials and argue about why each one is a quality product.

But, Hank has far more in mind than these individual product features. The One-Eyed Pirate, a large national seafood restaurant chain, has opened a franchise a few blocks down the road. It has an appealing theme that focuses on spicy, blackened dishes and a big-budget advertising campaign that challenges diners to be tough enough to handle the fiery food. Recently, The One-Eyed Pirate has taken a serious bite out of Hank's business. Hank knows that part of this is just the novelty of a new competitor, and his primary interest (his CSF) is to recapture some of the clientele he's lost and even bring in new diners.

If we take the time to sit down and listen to Hank's concerns, we can help him meet his needs while simultaneously improving our own sales. Rather than just pitching each individual product, we can come up with a package of spicy appetizers that will compete with the One-Eyed Pirate's. We can help him formulate a promotional campaign that will directly target his competitor—and, in the process, help sell more of our product. What we have done is to avoid simply focusing on making the sale and to begin working in a part-nership with Hank. By considering his CSFs, we have helped him achieve his own goals and simultaneously taken a step toward achieving our own.

Of course, in most businesses in today's market, we are not selling to a single outlet, and buying decisions are not made by only one specific individual within a company. Purchasing occurs at many different levels within the customer's company structure. Identifying the best individuals to approach is essential for effective sales. Salespeople often assume that certain individuals—high-level administrators and upper management—are out of reach and do not attempt to contact them. These assumptions can be harmful, though. Many people that we assume are impossible to reach are merely difficult to reach. Making the extra effort to contact them can really pay off.

It is advantageous to try to sell to the highest possible level in the customer's organizational chart so that the purchasing decisions will affect as many divisions and branches as possible. But, the power structure of a company is not the same as its organizational chart. An individual's position in terms of rank and seniority is not necessarily the same as his or her influence or power. The actual makeup of this power structure may not be easily available to us, but through our relationships with individuals within the customer's organization, we can begin to understand how that company is actually structured and how it works internally. Don't neglect individuals who are low in the structure, however. Not only do they often have more influence than it initially seems, but also they can help you learn the ins and outs of the company.

We need to invest time in learning the business concerns of people at all levels of the customer's company. We need to understand the CSFs at the major levels of the organization. We need to move up, down, and around to uncover the customer's needs and interests. This means understanding their business, their market, and their industry. We can begin by reading up on the industry's trade journals and talking to individual customers about the industry as a whole. Then we need to develop a guide for learning about the customer's own company so that we will know enough about it (and the community it is in) before we begin selling.

The planning guides that follow provide basic models for learning about a customer's business and uncovering the ways we can best meet their specific needs. Set them up on your laptop computer, in file folders, loose-leaf binders, or in any manner that best suits your working habits. They are meant only to help you get started thinking, learning, and growing with the customer. Please add to the categories and develop your own planning guides. Once filled in, they will form invaluable databases for use in developing sales strategies and planning sales calls.

Customer Guides
for Strategic Planning

Overall Information

Customer Profile:

Alliances:

Customer's Vision/Overall Goals:

Key Departments/Services:

Key People/Contacts:

Key Competition:

Customer's Major Business Issues/Challenges:

Sales Information

Customer's Target Market/Demographics:

Customer's Competitive Advantages:

Product Sales Figures:

Competitors' Product Sales:

Our Major Supporters for this Customer:

Major Supporters for the Competition:

Key Influences:

Our Obstacles to Product Success:

Factors for Approaching The Customer

Product Benefits of Priority to the Customer:

Needs of the Customer:

Value-Added Services We Have to Offer:

Business Needs of the Customer that Our Value Added Services Can Assist:

Resources We Need:

Decisions-Making Process:

How We Will Follow Up and Ensure Customer Satisfaction:

How To Measure Customer Satisfaction:

What We Are Doing to Build Supportive Relationships with Customer:

The key to becoming customer-focused is making the effort to stop thinking about individual products and begin thinking about the customer as a whole. We must learn as much as we can about the customer, his or her company, and his or her industry. We must concentrate on building effective, supportive relationships with the customer. We must analyze and plan the most effective way to reach our customers' needs. We must commit ourselves to genuinely helping our customers achieve success. This takes a lot more effort than merely selling the old way, but the conditions of today's market demand it. Changing how we think about customers will lead not only to better sales numbers but also increased satisfaction with our roles as salespeople and managers.

An Illustration of Effective Customer Focus

I have recently had the pleasure of seeing improved customer focus provide a real uplift in spirit to a salesperson that I'm currently working with. In addition, his sales and bottom-line results have dramatically increased.

When Alan (as I'll call him) took over his territory in January, his company was beginning to experience a sales decrease in two accounts for its major product. By June, this product's sales had dropped 38.2% in one account and 33.3% in the other. Alan was struggling, and he needed to take steps to improve his sales performance.

The first thing he did was to define the competitive problem that was causing the sales drop. He learned who the supporters of the competition were, and he performed a thorough analysis of each customer. Though he was new to the company, Alan was an experienced salesperson. He was familiar with a wide range of sales techniques and knew how to interact with the customer on a personal level. What he lacked was experience in selling this particular type of product and selling it to companies as large as those two accounts.

I worked with Alan to complete an analysis of his strengths and weaknesses. We utilized our "Process for Learning, Sharing, and Selling" to help define opportunities for improving customer satisfaction. Alan then developed a customer planning guide for each of the accounts.

Since he was new to the division, Alan was unsure whether he had relationships established firmly enough for him to approach the customers effectively. So we devised a team approach, in which a more experienced salesperson assisted Alan on each account. Alan soon recognized that it was necessary to move up the power structure and start talking with and selling to the executive level of each customer.

We brainstormed possible approaches for calling on the executives at these two companies and uncovering their critical success factors. As Alan said, "I couldn't even imagine approaching a C.E.O. before!" But he felt that we were committed to developing new services to better meet the needs of our customers and that we could do so if we could identify such opportunities. We planned the calls all the way down to specific questions. Alan contacted an executive secretary and found himself scheduled to meet the C.E.O. of one of the accounts.

Alan was surprised at how open this C.E.O. was to discussing his company's critical success factors. Today, Alan is working to meet the C.E.O.'s most important need, working at the top level of the account. At the same time, Alan learned from the director of the customer's most important department what that department's critical success factors were. One of these factors was the need to streamline the number of products they were stocking and using. We were able to locate an outside consultant to advise the director on facilitating this process. The department later hired this consultant on a permanent basis. By working with the C.E.O. and the department director, we greatly enlarged our understanding of and service to this key account. It turned into a win-win situation for Alan, for the company, and for the customer.

By using methods of customer focus, Alan and his team were well on the way to reversing the downward trend in sales for their major product. The account's positive response to Alan's initiative left little doubt that they would continue to view his company and team as providing outstanding customer service and satisfaction. Alan was soon promoted to team leader for the two accounts, and all three members of the teams were recognized in their Business Unit's newsletter for their accomplishments and for helping one another. (They also received a financial Special Achievement Award.) By the following June, Alan was seeing a 47.3% sales increase in one account and an 18.8% increase in the other. Customer focus really paid off.

Teamwork

Some people claim that most of history's great ideas and accomplishments have come from individuals, not groups or committees or teams. They refer to figures such as Einstein, Churchill, and Pasteur. They say that entrepreneurship is limited to individuals: one-person companies that have single leadership, can make quick decisions, and are not encumbered with details and committees. The Horatio Alger stories are encouraging to us, their biographies inspirational. We are brought up to believe we can do whatever we want singlehandedly, that it is our individual strengths that will move us along our journey.

This tradition of independence makes us prize our independence, and rightly so. Independence is wonderful. Gaining our independence is how we develop some of our real strengths: initiative, goal setting, time management, and decision making, just to name a few. The desire for independence, however, can also prevent us from recognizing our highest need and our most important asset: other people.

It has been said that the most important ability is the ability to work with others. Whether we are a small company with only a handful of employees or a very large corporation with thousands of people, the need for real teamwork is present. The individual entrepreneur needs the help of other people, whether they work for him or her, or whether they provide services, or whether they are just available. Entrepreneurs need other people. At the very least, they need customers, or there would be no one to buy their products or services.

For a sales division to function at maximum effectiveness, it needs to commit itself to fostering and developing teamwork, both within the company and outside of it. A team is a group of two or more people who are enhancing each other's strengths, who are learning and achieving more together than they would alone. They are synergistic: the whole is more effective than the individual parts. The individuals are growing more than they would alone. The team is helping to pull individuals to new heights, and its individuals are pulling the team to new heights. There is a commitment by the individual to the team and a commitment by the team to each individual.

A work group that is functioning well as a team will be committed to the goals that they have set together. They will know their individual roles and their responsibility for helping others on the team. They will be held accountable not only for their own personal performance but for the performance of the team as well.

One of the most important features of teamwork is that, unlike the traditional way of doing business, decisions are not dictated from the top down. Company employees of all levels work together to make decisions about the direction in which they move. As I learned during my years before coming to the Sunshine Division, the salespeople often have the best ideas on how to improve a division's performance. They are, after all, out in the field and in contact with the customers day in and day out. Rather than talking so much, a sales manager should learn to listen to the people in his group. His role should be to foster and coordinate communication among salespeople, to encourage them to work together.

It is important to include our customers in our teamwork as well. Who, after all, are customers? Are they not other people? Don't we first have to sell ourselves and be accepted before we can sell our product or services? If we do this, we will have people who accept us and trust us, and some of them would take a sincere interest in helping us—if we just ask. Why not form a team with our customers? When we think of customers only as people who will buy our product, we are failing to recognize that they can give us something more than money. Many customers are interested in providing feedback to help us shape our programs and in being of whatever assistance they can to improve the way we do business. We can form top achieving teams with such customers.

Certain people, admittedly, do not want to be a part of a team. They include:

- the loner— he doesn't need anybody
- the doer—he'd rather get all the credit for himself
- the wrecker—he likes to manipulate
- the user—he'd rather take
- the pleaser—he'd rather be heard
- the mover—he doesn't have time

Fundamentally, all these people are scared. They are motivated by fear and a lack of something they need. It could be that they want independence so much that they do not see the value of and the need for others. It could be that at this point in their development they have not had the opportunity to serve on an effective team. Or perhaps they have had a bad experience with being a part of a destructive group in the past. Whatever the reason for their reluctance, reality dictates that they will become part of our team. Then it's up to us, with patience and forgiveness—and with an awareness of why some of us don't really appreciate teamwork—to bring these people successfully into our new groups.

We must ensure that our team functions as well as possible, which means formulating standards for assessing the performance and effectiveness of an existing team:

- do we have a vision?
- do we have goals and objectives?
- do we have a plan?
- do our individual visions, goals, and objectives support the team?
- do different leaders emerge at different times and places?
- are we growing as a team and individually?
- are we taking risks?
- do we avoid blindly punishing failure?
- are we learning?
- are we celebrating?
- are we supportive of each other and our customers?
- are we sharing with others?
- are we having fun?
- are we improving?
- are we productive?
- are we contributing?
- are we listening?

Each team should agree upon its own performance standards and have criteria for measuring how well it is meeting these standards.

If I had to pick an ideal team, it would consist of three to twelve people with different backgrounds and experiences, different personalities, and different strengths. If a work group is too large, problems develop that prevent everyone from contributing and participating fully. A team that is too large runs the risk of being dominated by a small number of people, which defeats the purpose. Diversity is an asset to a smaller group because of each member's varying insights and experiences. I'm speaking not only of gender and race—which are what is usually meant by "diversity"—but also of the different personalities, learning styles, and life experiences that individuals can bring to the group. A team member who spent a number of years working overseas, for example, can contribute fresh ideas about how businesses in other countries operate.

For my team, I would want people with the ability to:

- care
- share
- commit
- initiate
- think
- join
- entertain new ideas
- work
- lead
- organize
- listen
- trust
- communicate
- sell
- grow

Most importantly, they would have the ability to forgive themselves and others for not being perfect. Some people have more talents, skills, and abilities than others, but all of us have enough to do a good job, to grow, and to move to another level of performance. We are all given the ability to care and forgive and to be happy. We need only to develop our true understanding of our role and function as an individual, and then we will be able to clearly see our role and function within our families, our work, and our communities.

Approaching our sales staff as a team is an important step in reaching the Q-factor.

Developing a Vision for the Group

"You are not here merely to make a living. You are here in order to enable the world to live more amply, with greater vision, with a finer spirit of hope and achievement. You are here to enrich the world, and you impoverish yourself if you forget the errand."

—Woodrow Wilson

Once you have dedicated yourself to the principles of teamwork, you must create and implement a vision of what you want your organization to be. To be successful as an individual you need a personal vision of who you want to be; similarly, a company or work group needs a vision of what it wants to be. A vision is about greatness. It expresses our values and what we hope to contribute. It comes from the heart. A vision must focus on service, on adding value, and on empowering others. It spells out our highest ideals and wishes. Great visions are created and shaped in partnership, by those who will be living the vision.

A vision is not a plan of action. When taking a trip, you cannot plan out your route until you know what city you want to end up in. The same is true for running a business. Before you can begin making changes within your group and within your company, you must first formulate and recognize your broadest, most long-term goals.

To develop this vision, it is important that everyone on the team understands what a vision and mission statement are. With the Sunshine Division, I first held a brief meeting and discussed our need to develop a team vision. I later sent out several articles to the salespeople to give them some preliminary ideas with which to work. These articles included James J. Mapes' "Foresight First," Ken Blanchard's "Great Leaders Serve With Vision and Implementation," and the Ford Motor Company's "Petersen's Six-Stage Process For Transforming a

Company's Culture." We also watched as a group Joel Barker's videotape, "The Power of Vision." Although they did not deal directly with sales and sales divisions, these resources provided helpful ideas for getting started, and I would recommend them for your team as well.

In two meetings, one in June and another in September, we got together to formulate the initial vision for our division. Working in small groups of three or four salespeople at the June meeting, we first sat down and tried to identify what we considered to be our greatest strengths as a division. We then brought the small groups together, compared our responses, and selected the strengths that were most frequently named by the individual groups.

The strengths most often mentioned included:

- acceptance and openness to new ways of doing things
- supporting one another's efforts
- creativity and innovation
- having fun
- focusing on what is important
- knowing how to help each other
- improvement by teamwork and sharing
- willingness to take risks

Everyone on the team was also given an assignment to take back home in order to get them thinking about their individual roles within the group—in other words, to help them develop their individual visions. Each salesperson was asked to answer the following questions:

1. What do we want to become in our present jobs?
2. What do we want to be able to do in our present job?
   For our division?
   For our company?
3. What do we want to become for our customers?
4. What is our purpose in our work?

Each salesperson was asked to write out his/her answers to these questions and to bring them to our next team meeting. They were also asked to think of any pictures, photographs, or symbols that might help communicate their vision to themselves.

At the next meeting, we again broke into subgroups of three or four people each to discuss the individual visions and to make a list of the phrases or words that they found themselves using in common. Each subgroup reported back to the team as a whole, and we compiled the lists of common words and phrases into one large list. We drew on this list to construct a vision statement: a concise expression of the team's overall purpose and goals.

The statement we came up with was brief but memorable:

> *Our vision is to break through previously-defined limitations, to explore new frontiers for personal growth, and to boldly go where no division has gone before.*

It is helpful to express your vision not only in lists and paragraphs but in a concise, visually-appealing form. (That's where asking the salespeople to think about pictures or photographs comes in.) Our vision statement was accompanied by an illustration of a rocket ship with our major products and our division number displayed on the side. This flagship was bursting through clouds that represented limitations and heading toward the stars.

You could laugh and say that such an image is hokey and corny. What, after all, do pictures of rocket ships and clouds have to do with improving sales? What is truly important, however, is not the image itself but rather what the image represents: the belief that a vision developed by a group can be an inspiration and a reminder to head in the direction in which they want to move. The image of our vision served as a quick, effective way to express our goals and make them memorable.

> **Theorem:** An organizational vision will be successful if the team vision is part of the organizational vision. The team vision will be successful if the individual vision is part of the team vision. All persons who want to be empowered must first be committed to taking ownership of their jobs and creating a personal vision.

Once you have formulated your vision, it is essential that you keep it continually in front of your team so that you never lose sight of your overall objectives. You must be creative to do so. Each Sunshine Division salesperson had a three-ring binder with the image of our vision on the outside cover and organized by division/territory plans, products, quality and sales figures. Inside the binder were pages for note taking. Each of these pages had the image of our vision printed on it. We also printed the image on smaller pads for team members to keep beside their phones in their homes so that it would be easy to jot down ideas. Whenever they made small contributions and achievements, I sent the salespeople specially-made thank-you notes with the vision image printed on the cards and envelopes. These steps helped ensure that our vision would always be alive and on the minds of team members.

A vision for your team is essential. It must be reached cooperatively, be agreed upon by all team members, and can never be forgotten as you go about making more focused, daily-level changes.

Breaking Through Limitations

Before a team can begin trying to reach its vision, it must first identify the limitations that are currently holding it back. Each person must understand what barriers and obstacles lie in the path of progress before he or she can move down that path. Sometimes these limitations are real to a person only because of that person's perceptions, but we know that perceptions can often be as influential and restraining as reality. Identifying limitations also provides feedback from the group to the manager on what he or she may be focusing on to the detriment of the individuals and the team. You can't knock down barriers until you are aware that they exist.

It is often helpful to team members to see that others may not perceive the same limitations they do. Simply talking about an obstacle can sometimes make it go away (or at least lessen its importance.) One member of a sales group, for example, may feel that there is too much competitive pressure within the division, that one salesperson can succeed only at another's expense. This perceived atmosphere may be hindering his doing the best job he can: he's too busy looking over his shoulder to concentrate fully on what the customer needs. Just talking this concern out with his team members may convince him that the group atmosphere is more supportive and less competitive than he thought. Simple conversation has eliminated one limitation.

Of course, many of the barriers to success cannot be overcome merely through discussion, but your division or work group can certainly take steps to lessen the problem. When your team is working together to identify these limitations, some of the most important things to think about are the obstacles to:

- increasing customer satisfaction
- increasing sales
- improving productivity
- getting more meaning/enjoyment from our work

As with developing the team vision, I have found that splitting up into small groups of three or four is the most effective way to generate useful ideas. Small groups foster a sense of openness and candor that is often missing from larger meetings. Once the small groups have come up with their answers, combine them all together, selecting the most common responses, and from that pin down what your group feels to be its most serious barriers.

The following list gives some of the limitations the Sunshine Division realized it would need to break through. As you read these items, consider whether any apply to you and/or your work group and contemplate how understanding them can help you overcome them:

- too much stress placed on sales figures
- too much emphasis on a set number of customer calls each day
- failure to take action on specifics
- unreasonable expectations of market share
- failure to comprehend the amount of influence we have on our customers, on our sales, and on one another
- fear of failure and risks
- prejudgment of customers without seeing them and understanding them
- dependence upon one-product success

With these limitations on the table in front of us, The Sunshine Division could begin to address them and eliminate them.

Acting on the Vision

Once team members know where they want to go, it's time to develop an overall plan of action that establishes how they will go about achieving their vision. This plan provides a framework for the team's daily operations.

When developing your overall plan of action, it is important to keep your vision firmly in mind while looking also at the obstacles that stand in the way. Be sure to use as many resource materials as you can and modify their ideas to meet your specific circumstances. The Sunshine Division, for example, began with Deming's Fourteen Points for the Transformation of Management. We knew that not all the points would work for us, since they were designed more for industry than for sales, but we took those which we thought relevant and adapted them to specifically meet our needs. We also considered recent changes in our marketplace and in our company and tried to envision what type of working environment we wanted to be a part of.

When a company or work group is going through a lot of rapid changes, I would recommend an Opinion Survey to help identify team members' current views of the working environment and to pinpoint what needs to be improved. If you have the time and money, numerous outside consulting firms can conduct these surveys for you and provide a response that not only is comprehensive but also, since it encourages openness through anonymity, is more revealing than surveys conducted in team meetings. Once you have compiled this data, you are ready to develop the overall plan. Our plan was as follows:

The Sunshine Division's 10-Point Plan for Continuing Improvement of Quality for Increased Productivity

1. Create constancy of purpose for improvement. Quality will become our focus along with results and fun.
2. We will strive for developing long-term relationships built upon trust and service to our customers.

3. Training and opportunities to learn and grow will be avail-. able to each individual based upon interest and need.

4. We will take responsibility for helping each other do a better job.

5. We will increase our feeling of being secure by risk taking and creatively rewarding failure.

6. We will improve our teamwork within our division and the home office staff (our internal customers).

7. All goals will contain a description of how they are going to be accomplished.

8. We will assure that our major job skills are defined as to what is and is not acceptable in terms of quality.

9. We will encourage and reward reporting of problems, barriers, ideas, decisions, limitations, and recommendations to improve quality.

10. We will continue acquiring new information and the skills required to deal with improving quality and increasing results.

This plan became the framework for all the changes we would later implement. It helped keep us focused on our goals of continued improvement of quality, increased productivity, new dollar growth, and job enjoyment— all while controlling costs. A similar plan can do the same for your division or work group.

Focusing on Strengths

Once you have your overall plan, you need to focus on the strengths of your group. Looking for strengths is far more rewarding than looking for weaknesses. It helps instill confidence in team members and gets the group off on a positive note. Consider the successes that the work group has achieved in the recent past. Look for any differentiating factors between your team and other teams within your company, factors which give your team an individual identity and have made members feel a sense of success. Consider, as well, the experience, skills, activities, and knowledge of each individual member. From all these ideas you can pull together a list of the overall strengths that will help you achieve your goals.

We decided to concentrate on improving quality through the following eight demonstrated strengths:

1. Quality Sales Calls / Expansion and Retention
2. Quality Customer Service / Customer Satisfaction
3. Quality Group Selling Activities
4. Increased Customer Office Calls
5. Quality Statistical Control / Feedback
6. Communication / Teamwork
7. Creating opportunities from awareness of competitive activities
8. Performance reviews which include acceptance of problem definition and recognition of specific accomplishments.

The accomplishment of our goals required thinking in new ways about quality, systems, and our own jobs. New relationships had to be forged between people. Quality had to be all-pervasive—the driving force of change. Only then were we on the path to reaching our vision to break through previously defined limitations, to explore new frontiers for personal growth, and to boldly go where no division has gone before. The *10-Point Plan,* along with the *8 Strengths* became our framework for building an environment and culture for implementing our T.Q.M. philosophy and our Continuous Quality Initiative.

Shifting the Paradigm

The second of Dr. Deming's 14 Points is to adopt a new philosophy of management. This means shifting the paradigm on which your group and your company operate. A paradigm is a typical or clear pattern; in a business, it is a universally-accepted model of doing work. In his book *Future Edge,* Joel Barker defines a paradigm as "a set of rules and regulations (written or unwritten) that does two things: (1) it establishes or defines boundaries; and (2) it tells you how to behave inside the boundaries in order to be successful."

Companies often operate the way they do simply because that is the way they've always operated. Their paradigms are so deeply entrenched that innovations are difficult to achieve. In order to implement a new way of doing business, then, we must first analyze what our current rules and regulations are, whether written or unwritten. In fact, the unwritten are often the most rigid: employees can be governed by them without even realizing they exist. It's just "how business is done." Once we identify the rules and assumptions under which we have been operating, we can then "shift the paradigm" to make possible changes and improvements. As Barker has written, "a paradigm shift is a change to a new game, a new set of rules."

The world of track and field provides an illuminating example. For decades high jumpers used the "straddle" technique: a jumper approached the bar at a forty-five degree angle, jumped off his inside foot, then brought his outside leg up and over so that he rolled over the bar with his stomach downward. This technique was the unwritten but accepted way to compete in the high jump. Then in the 1960's Dick Fosbury had a better idea. Rather than being at a sharp angle, Fosbury's path of approach was almost parallel to the bar. He twisted when he jumped, turning his back to the bar. He went over headfirst, his stomach facing upward, and flopped so that his shoulders hit the mat first. In the process he handily defeated old-style jumpers and won the gold medal in the 1968 Olympics. The "Fosbury flop" was, by the letter of the rules, legal, but it raised howls of protest from other competitors who claimed that it was against the spirit of the high jump. After considerable controversy, Fosbury's method was approved by track and field's governing bodies. It is now the standard high jump technique and has pushed the world record over a foot higher than it was during the straddle-style days.

Dick Fosbury successfully shifted the paradigm of the high jump. We must do the same thing in business.

Not long after we laid out our 10-point plan, the Sunshine Division began shifting our own paradigm. I participated in a seminar led by Conway Quality, Inc. called "Paradigms Shift and The Right Way To Manage." Later, I read Joel Barker's *Future Edge*. Both sources provided solid ideas for changing the way the Sunshine Division operated. I was not trying to be a maverick or a "cop-fighter," but I was trying to lead a charge to change our rules and regulations because the customers were changing. Today's customers are more demanding. Everybody wants a better price. Accessibility to customers is more limited. More buying and purchasing is being done by committees, competition has increased, and decisions are being made by the people at the top of the customers' organizations. The cost of doing business is escalating, and salespeople, managers, and companies are getting scared and uptight because they feel they are losing control. The old ways are not working as well, and oftentimes people don't know what to do.

When the Sunshine Division found that doing the same things we used to do was no longer getting a good result, we knew it was time for change.

Using ideas from the Conway seminar, we outlined our Old vs. New Paradigm Characteristics:

Old	New
• Authoritative	• Participative
• Use of threat	• Reinforcement
• Management as the expert	• Salespeople doing the job are the experts
• Fear of blame	• Openness
• Good enough	• Continuous improvement
• Selling to customers	• Partnership with customers
• Quality in numbers	• Quality determined by customers
• Individuals rewarded	• Individuals and teams rewarded
• Emphasis on results	• Emphasis on improved process
• Quality versus quantity	• Customer satisfaction
• Individuals solving problems	• Teams solving problems
• Driven by sales performance	• Driven by return on investment
• Short-term planning	• Long and short-term planning

Taken together, these characteristics provide new and better guidance for doing business in today's market. They offer direction both for sales managers and salespeople and are applicable to almost all sales organizations.

As with all the ideas presented in this book, it is not enough simply to announce that you are changing your paradigm and let it go at that. There must be periodic assessments of how well you are meeting your goals. To help us evaluate our improvement, the Sunshine Division took anonymous evaluations every four months to determine where we were as a group in our paradigm shift. At each of our team meetings, which we held every four months, we scheduled time for training and education on Continuous Quality Improvement. During this time, we

took anonymous evaluations of how each member of the team
. felt we were progressing toward shifting our paradigm.

Each person rated the individual factors of the paradigm shift
(such as moving from authoritative to participative, threat to
reinforcement) and then rated the shift as a whole. We used a
simple scale of zero to ten, with ten being the highest rating:

0-2:   no change
3-4:   some change, but not consistent
5-6:   change with moderate consistency
7-8:   highly-consistent change
9-10: complete change

When we checked in January, our rating was 5.5 out of 10. By
September we had moved up to a 6.0, and we made it our goal
to reach at least 7.0 by the following January. We knew we
wouldn't reach perfection immediately—all change takes
time—but we were moving steadily in the right direction.

Shifting Individuals' Paradigms

After you have made progress as a group, it is time to move to
the individual level. Have the members of your team identify
how a) they operated individually under the old group paradigm and b) how they should operate under the new rules and
regulations brought forth by the team paradigm shift. By this
point, each member knows the changes necessary within the
team as a whole, and each knows the changes necessary in
management. Now they can look at themselves and identify
what changes they need to make on a personal level.

The Sunshine Division salespeople got together and identified the following old vs. new paradigm characteristics:

Old: Focus on number of calls/presentations
New: Focus on relationships with and service to customers to
increase sales

Old: Forty hours/week
New: Do whatever it takes to make a positive impact on customers

Old: Work with manager to be evaluated on progress
New: Work with manager to learn, share, and develop strengths

Old: Focus on territory/individual achievement
New: Focus on group, team, and individual achievement

Old: Commitment to sales
New: Commitment to quality and service. Sales will naturally follow.

Old: Focusing on weaknesses & problems
New: Focusing on strengths & solutions

Old: See ancillary customers only when needed
New: Establish constant working relationships with customers

Old: Individualism
New: Team orientation

Old: Short-Term Sales
New: Long-Term relationships

Old: Given number of contacts per day
New: Contacting customers who make a difference

Old: Sales-oriented
New: Customer-oriented

4

PART FOUR

Processes and Process Variation

Becoming Process-Oriented

"If you don't have the outcomes you want—change the process/improve the process."

– W. Edwards Deming

One of the most important elements of the paradigm shift needed by today's sales forces is changing from a results orientation to a process orientation. W. Edwards Deming defines quality as "a never ending cycle of constant improvement." Continuous improvement is a process-oriented, rather than a results-oriented way of thinking.

Too many of us in management and sales tend to look only at bottom-line results, and not enough time is spent developing and improving processes. The dictionary defines process as:

1. *a system of operation in the production of something, 2. a series of actions or functions that bring about an end or result.*

It is time to begin focusing on processes in our businesses. We have become so accustomed to "putting out fires", pushing for results, and accepting rework and waste that we often ignore the process (or lack thereof) by which we achieve the outcomes we want and need. We want the big sale and the quick increase in market share so much that we've forgotten the value of cumulative improvements. In doing so, we tend to measure and reward only bottom-line numbers and not actual progress. By focusing solely on our desire to make big increases in sales we often miss out on small, every-day improvements.

With processes, the focus is on improving *how* work gets done. If we focus on improving the processes that serve customers, the sales results will take care of themselves. If we give customer-concerns top priority and develop and improve processes that provide services to our customers, then bottom-line sales numbers will naturally rise. We will also be in the position of providing a service that surprises customers by how well it meets their needs—even needs that they were not aware of.

Let's take the classic simplified business example: a child's lemonade stand. The young entrepreneur finds out that a competing stand down the street is selling a sweeter type of lemonade that customers like better. Being results-oriented, our entrepreneur decides to add 33% more sugar to his recipe. The customers like the new, sweeter product, and the stand's sales jump 20%. Adding more sugar, however, raises operating costs, so the stand's net profit increases only 2%. Still, results-oriented thinking worked, right?

A process-oriented entrepreneur would approach the challenge differently. Rather than jumping to a bottom-line decision, he first looks at the process by which his lemonade is sweetened and asks, "Can I make that process more efficient?" He discovers that while mixing the lemonade in his kitchen, he tends to spill sugar all over the counter because his measuring cup does not have an easy-pouring spout. He switches measuring cups and finds that 33% more sugar is going into each pitcher. His product is sweeter, and—without an increase in raw material cost—his sales jump 20%. And his profits jump even more.

When you think about it, virtually everything you do in life is a process: brushing your teeth in the morning, deciding what to wear, driving to work. All these processes can be analyzed and broken down into their individual steps. Explicit thought about these steps is an effective tool for increasing how well you perform each process. We are surrounded by processes within our businesses as well: the collection of market and sales data, making sales calls, assessing individuals' performance, hiring and training. By looking closely at the processes of business, we can begin to see ways to improve them.

The danger, of course, is in focusing solely on processes at the expense of profits. We can get so wrapped up in analyzing the inner workings of our group that we forget our overall purpose: selling products. But, I submit that you do not have to choose between a process-oriented and a results-oriented way of thinking. You can achieve both, and you need to achieve both. The odds are, however, that the best opportunity for bottom-line improvement lies with improving the processes by which your team or company operates: the process for achieving customer satisfaction; the process for learning the customer's needs, wants, and expectations; the process for sharing information and knowledge; the process for selling. If we address these processes from both points of view, we will move towards our vision and exceed our goals.

Deming says you can tell that you are into continuing improvement when you start thinking about and working with processes. Examining processes can help pull a team together and stimulate creativity. Decision-making is improved because decisions are based more on data and information and not on guesswork or a gut feeling. We live and work in an age of information and knowledge. Knowledge is power, but knowledge about knowledge is more powerful.

The FOCUS Process Improvement Strategy

One of the basic process-improvement methods the Sunshine Division worked with was **FOCUS:**

Find a process to improve

Organize a team that knows the process

Clarify current knowledge of the process

Understand causes of process variation

Select the process improvement

FOCUS provides a step-by-step method for beginning to improve individual processes in your work group.

F

*F*ind a Process to Improve

Generally, select a process that has a heavy impact on your performance indicators. The following are good criteria for selecting a process to improve:

- Processes critical for sales.
- Processes important to meeting the needs and expectations of customers.
- Processes costing you money by not meeting goals.
- Processes causing you problems or pain.
- Very complicated processes.

For a sales group, one of the most useful areas to improve is the selling process for an individual product—particularly one which meets some or all of the criteria above.

As we began implementing our quality initiative program, the Sunshine Division selected our best-selling product for a Process Improvement study. Though we had a larger market share for that product than any of our competitors, sales had been slipping recently, and many people in our company thought we had reached a plateau beyond which we could not improve. As I will discuss later, our Process Improvement results proved that theory wrong.

O

Organize a Team That Knows the Process

One of the best ways to improve your company's or work group's processes is to assemble a Process Improvement Team. There are several benefits for using the teamwork approach:

- Teams can be a quick and economical way to define processes and improve them.
- Teams offer an opportunity for continued training and learning for their members.
- Teams can encourage others to use the improved processes and take advantage of the opportunities for growth.
- Teams can create opportunities for group and individual empowerment by including nonmanagerial personnel in the decision-making process.
- By encouraging participation and the input of salespeople's opinions, teams help change an organization's or work group's culture from top-down to participatory management.

The end result is not only a more efficient way of doing business but also a better atmosphere for the salespeople in your group.

For your team, select people who have particularly valuable knowledge of the process as well as people having different skills, abilities, knowledge, and experience. Diversity is a key to effective analysis and solutions: people from varying backgrounds approach problems differently, ensuring maximum creativity within the team. In addition, you may want to invite people from outside the work group who are customers (internal or external) who you believe will add knowledge or be important to the improvement plan.

These people constitute your Improvement Team for that particular process. Their goals should be:

- to improve processes by clarifying purposes, constructing flow charts, reducing variation
- to teach the use of process improvement methods
- to identify opportunities for improvement for themselves, for others within the group, and for management
- to work on a variety of projects having differing team members, tasks, deadlines, and goals

For this team to work, there must be trust among members. Factors that help build trust include:

- having clear goals and purpose
- being open, candid, and willing to listen
- being decisive and supporting decisions
- supporting all team members
- taking responsibility and assuming accountability
- giving credit to team members
- trusting team members and respecting their opinions
- recognizing that not everyone needs to be on a team

To get started, a Process Improvement Team should be assembled from both volunteers and persons appointed by the manager. After they understand the goals and purposes of the team, members then need to select a team leader from among themselves. Team meetings should be held about once a month in the beginning. This interval is long enough to avoid interrupting the regular flow of daily business but frequent enough to make the results of the meetings effective. Later, after the group members have become situated, meetings can be held on an as-needed basis.

C

*C*larify *Current Knowledge of the Process*

One of the most effective ways to gain understanding of a process is to construct a flow chart. A flow chart is a pictorial summary of the operations that occur within a particular process. It helps create understanding by defining the scope of the process, locating starting points and end-points, distinguishing decision-making steps from action steps, identifying opportunities for improvements, reducing variation, and depicting how tasks are related and grouped in sequence to accomplish a particular set of outcomes.

Construct one chart on the process as it currently exists. Break down the entire process into its necessary components. Doing this takes some thought and a little creativity. There are often small details that you might not think of right off. Be sure to involve each member of your Process Improvement Team in the brainstorming step. The more eyes you bring to the subject, the more perspectives you'll have.

There are many ways to construct a flow chart, but one of the simplest uses the following four basic symbols:

• The Oval: ⬭

Ovals indicate input or output points in the process, such as where a customer order is received or a memo is sent out. Ovals are also used to indicate the beginning and ending of a process.

• The Rectangle: ▭

Rectangles represent specific steps within the overall process that lead to only one outcome.

• The Diamond: ◇

Diamonds indicate a decision step in the process and generally lead to two or more outcomes, depending on the results of that decision.

• The Arrow: ⇒

Arrows represent the paths in the process, linking the various ovals, diamonds, and rectangles. The point on the arrow indicates the direction in which the process flows.

Let's look at an example of the ways in which these symbols are used to construct a flow chart. An entrepreneur runs a small business that sells tee shirts at local sporting events. He decides to analyze the way in which he goes about selecting each event and setting up his stand. Here's how his flow chart might look:

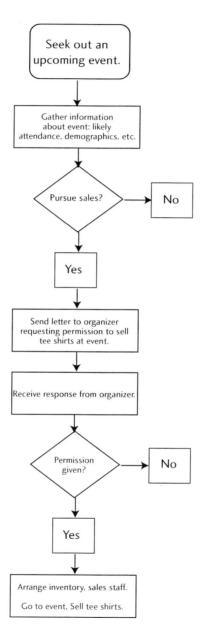

The chart above is simplified, of course. Each of the ovals and rectangles can be broken down into smaller processes and outlined in their own flow charts. The more detailed your analysis and flow chart, the better your understanding of the overall process will be.

The following flow chart is more complicated and details the process of selling machine tools to industrial manufacturers:

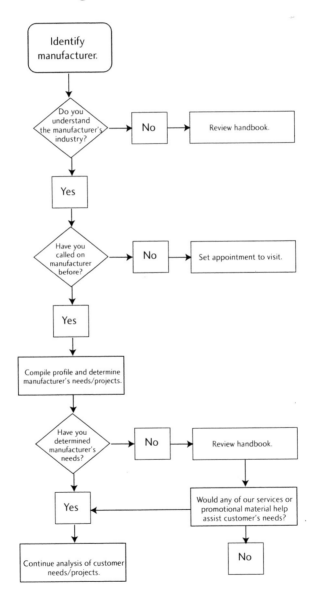

It is important that you try to make your flow chart depict as accurately as possible the way a specific process actually works in your company. Oversimplifying or recording the way it should be done rather than the way it actually is done will be counterproductive. Once the group has created a flow chart on the process as it is now, construct one showing the ideal process or the way the process would look if everything worked right. A careful look at the differences between the actual and ideal charts will reveal opportunities for improvement.

U

*U*nderstanding Variation

You are likely to learn—particularly when analyzing a process performed by more than one person—that more than one process occurs or that specific steps within the process vary from individual to individual. You should indicate variation in the process using a decision-diamond (i.e., you can choose to do it this way, or that.) These differences could very well be a source of variation in quality. While it is not necessary to force everyone to adhere rigidly to the same exact process, looking at variations within the flow chart is a good way to find opportunities to improve overall performance.

Understanding variation is important. When we don't:

- We see data and not trends.
- We take action where there are no trends.
- We see natural variation as special events.
- We blame others and give credit for things over which we have no control.
- We make ineffective efforts to improve.
- We can't project or plan for the future effectively.

To improve our processes, we must understand the causes of process variation. The dictionary defines variation as:

1) The act, process, or result of varying; change or deviation. 2) Something that is slightly different from another of the same type.

I like these definitions because variation exists in all aspects of our daily lives. There is variation among salespeople, managers, customers, and everyone else. We all have varying abilities to sell and manage or to perform any other task. There is variation among companies of the same size and in the same industry. We constantly make decisions based on our interpretation of the variation.

One of our responsibilities as salespeople and managers is to make decisions. These decisions are often based on how we interpret figures that are available to us about sales, expenses, budgets, customer call rates, etc. Let's imagine that for four months in a row our sales are below goal. Do the data indicate a trend? What action should be taken? Or, for example, let's suppose there are differences in the performance of territories and divisions. Who needs special attention? Who deserves recognition?

We must be able to determine whether the variation is a new trend or is similar to what has been seen in the past. This distinction is necessary to prevent:

- blaming people for problems beyond their control
- wasting time looking for explanations
- rewarding others when their performances do not warrant it
- taking action or changing direction when it would have been better to do nothing

or

- doing nothing when it would have been better to take action.

The performance of any process or system can be identified and measured. Admittedly, many of these processes do not reveal anything that can be easily counted. Still, performance measurements can be formulated.

Walter Shewhart says that the causes of variation within a process or system fall into two categories:

1. **Common Cause** (or assignable cause): Those causes that are inherently part of the process or systems day after day and affect everyone working within the process.

2. **Special Cause** (or chance cause): Those causes that are not part of the process all of the time, do not affect everyone, and arise because of specific circumstances.

For example, the participation of salespeople attending a division meeting is affected by causes that are common to all present, such as the agenda, room temperature, lighting, size of the room, and the skills of the moderator. There are also causes affecting participation that are special to each individual, such as lack of sleep, family problems, and health. If lack of participation is primarily due to common causes, then increased participation at future meetings of the same type will require action by the organizer or group leader. If lack of participation is due primarily to special causes, then increased participation will require action by the individuals in attendance. It's easy to see the importance of knowing whether the variation in the process is dominated by common or special causes before a manager assigns responsibility for improvement.

If your division is facing a sales problem—such as a leading product that is starting to dip in terms of total sales—some of these common causes may be at fault:

• product knowledge
• customer knowledge
• frequency of calls on the right customer
• presentation to needs/wants

• motivational factors for the sales force

Some special causes may be:
• health or personal problems
• errors in sales figures
• confusion over the sales process

Once you have identified the causes behind the variation, you can decide whether the variation is a problem and, if so, the steps that can be made to alleviate it. The remedy may require either changing the process as a whole (for common causes) or helping individual team members understand their function within the process (special causes).

In general, your Process Improvement Team should seek to reduce variation within the process it is studying. Certainly, all salespeople have their own way of doing things. The goal of process improvement is not to be restrictive or to force everyone into the same way of conducting business. One of the characteristics of an effective sales manager is the flexibility to allow his or her staff to operate in the way that best serves their capabilities and needs. Most often, however, your Process Improvement Teams will find that variation is not due to differences in individuals' capabilities and personalities but rather due to lack of a useful road map for doing business.

One of the effects of top-down, numbers-driven management is that salespeople are told only that they must achieve a particular goal and not how they are to achieve it. As a result, individual salespeople are left to discover their own techniques for making sales; they are, in other words, forced to formulate their own processes. Oftentimes, simply identifying how various members of a team handle each process can be enlightening for everyone. Team members can learn tricks from each other in a more formal way than merely talking shop over the water cooler. This is the type of variation that the process team is meant to reduce: variation caused by lack of experience or information.

Let's take an example from the pharmaceuticals sales field. The process team has identified regular sales calls as an important step in the overall sales process. When trying to determine how salespeople actually go about making these calls, the team has learned that each member has her/his own idea of which people within a hospital's organization to use as key contacts. Clearly there is variation within this particular stage of the process. If these key contacts are determined on the basis of personal relationships with hospital staff members, then the variation is a result of a specific cause: just because one salesperson has established a close relationship with a pharmacy director does not mean that every salesperson should go directly to the pharmacy directors in his or her region. But it is worth considering whether there is a more common cause at work in the process. Perhaps individuals have different lists of key contacts because of a lack of information, because they are not sure exactly whom they should be contacting. In such a case, developing a step-by-step checklist will not only reduce variation (in itself a trivial goal) but also will help improve the performance of each team member and the division as a whole, which is the whole point of the process-improvement method.

The purpose of understanding variation, in other words, is to learn how a particular process works and to decide what—if any—changes need to be made.

S

Select the Process Improvement

The ultimate—but not the only—criterion for selecting a means of improvement is the potential for satisfying customer needs and exceeding their expectations. Ideally, the process selected will be one in which there is considerable confusion about how each member of the team should operate. To return to the pharmaceutical example, if the improvement team decides that salespeople have differing ways of making contacts within hospitals and that this variation is due to the lack of coherent guidelines for making such contacts, then it will certainly be helpful to focus on the regular sales call process and attempt to improve it.

The improvement in such a situation may be as simple as assembling a checklist of possible contacts. This list can be compiled by surveying team members and learning from them the people with whom they have had the best success. The final checklist, which would be distributed among all the salespeople in the group, might look like this:

Whom should we be calling on regularly?
1. Pharmacy Department
   a. Director of Pharmacy
   b. Clinical Pharmacist
   c. Purchasing Agent
2. Key High Admitting Physicians
3. Antibiotic Sub-Committee Members
4. Clinical Nurse Managers
   a. Intensive Care Unit
   b. Orthopedic
   c. Medical/Surgical
5. Quality Assurance Registered Nurse
6. Microbiology
7. Discharge Coordinator
8. Chief Resident

This outline of the process is not rigid; a salesperson is not required to call upon each of these people while excluding all others. What the checklist provides is a standard way of doing business, a method by which the salespeople within the division can ensure that they are making the most of the regular sales calls.

This type of checklist can be adapted by salespeople in a wide variety of industries. By laying out the process specifically— down to step-by-step checklists of what can be and should be done—salespeople are given a clear, understandable method for performing their daily activities. With this understanding comes improved performance and, ultimately, an improved bottom line.

5

PART FIVE

The Q-Factor In Action

About the same time that our division underwent a major reorganization which replaced almost one third of the personnel in our group, our major product, the largest in dollar-volume and profit, slipped from a growth trend to a .7% shrinkage. Seventy percent of the territories were showing decreases that ranged from -6.4% to -44.4%, and despite our declines, the Sunshine Division's market share remained larger than other divisions' in the region and nation. Some people, both managers and sales reps, were saying that we had simply reached our peak and that since we had such a high share of market in the most competitive field in our industry (there were 16 companies competing with us in that product market) our goal would have to be simply to maintain our current volume and market share.

Our division, however, was determined to learn what it would take to get this number-one product back on a growth trend. We knew that once a product in our industry begins to lose sales in such a competitive environment, it is very rare for that product to turn around and get back on a growth curve. But we were going to try.

We planned two meetings in April for our new work group. The first was for new people coming into the group. I wanted them to get to know one another and have some exposure to me before our first meeting as a new division. The second meeting was for the group as a whole.

Coincidentally, the day before our first meeting, I attended a

Quality Seminar held by Dr. W. Edwards Deming in my home town. Later that evening I was sitting in the living room of my home, thinking that I would like to take something with me the next day that would be helpful for the new salespeople. So I took a yellow legal pad and jotted down a flow chart describing what I thought was necessary to learn and to do to increase sales and make customers happy with us and with our product.

I took this rough flow chart for learning and selling with me the next day to the meeting for incoming salespeople. At the end of the meeting, I told them that I hadn't wanted to come empty-handed, and I passed around the chart. I stressed that they shouldn't change any plans or modify the ways that they were working, but that I had written out something they could be thinking about. A lot of us salespeople and managers feel better if we have something in hand to leave with customers, and I wanted them to know I had put some special thought and effort into our first visit together. I learned several things:

1) Don't have a meeting that includes new members without getting to know the new people coming into the work group ahead of time. They appreciate the consideration, and everybody is more comfortable at the meeting.

2) If you have something that you think might help the sales-people, all you have to do is present it to them and give them the option of evaluating it. They will let you know whether it's helpful.

3) When you are thinking about being considerate to some-one else, sit down, take time in a comfortable spot with paper and pencil, and see what happens. Let the thoughts move you, and write down what comes into your head. Don't evaluate; just write. Something helpful may come from it, and you can refine it later.

The unsolicited feedback from the salespeople on the process and flow chart was very positive, and in June we started bringing the idea to life. Whenever we could work it in with our other priorities, we broke our division into smaller groups based on geographic locations. Our approach was to work one day at a time in these small groups. (Actually four or six hours a day was about all you could do to be creative and write down all of the details.) We were going to go with the idea of "an inch wide and a mile deep" rather than the opposite broad approach.

After meeting with one small group, I would then go to the next and present, in a typed format, the material the previous group had come up with. The current group would have to understand and agree with the information. If not, we would change and add to it; then the next group would go over this work, and so on until we completed the process. We finished the cycle in five months. Everyone in our division had contributed their ideas to the process, and it didn't take long to see that this was also a great training exercise and a way of pulling our new division together as a team.

This completed process, which we called "The Process for Learning, Sharing, and Selling," contained the following concepts:
- customer satisfaction
- learning the product
- learning the market
- learning the customer
- self-direction/self-management
- a "road-map" for finding opportunities for improvement and continuous improvement
- building supportive relationships
- reduction of waste (time, rework, resources)
- teamwork
- self-improvement/knowledge/training
- data collection
- vision and mission statement
- flow chart

The Payoff

The purpose of the Process for Learning, Sharing, and Selling was three-fold:

1) to achieve customer satisfaction
2) to increase productivity
3) to implement Continuous Quality Improvement

We aimed, in short, to do nothing less than bring the Q-factor—the ideas discussed in previous chapters in this book—into action within the Sunshine Division. It didn't take long before we began seeing the results.

One of the best ways to determine whether a new way of doing business is working is to get feedback from the people who are best able to judge the results: the salespeople. In December, we asked the members of our work group to write memos that evaluated their experiences working with the process. The following passages are taken from these memos:

"I focused on learning the customer portion of the process, this serves as a system to check my performance with the customer. The process forces you to think about where you are going and what you are doing. I view it as a kind of road map that guides me daily. I recently developed and prioritized my customer objectives following the guidelines provided by the process. I was also reminded by the process that learning the product is ongoing. This has inspired me to form a focus group with (another sales rep.) to review competitive activities and information, new articles, product user, and related issues. We will meet monthly."
— a salesperson with three years of experience.

"The process requires us to pay attention to details that may not be routine to us (i.e., requires more thoroughness.) For newer people—a process to follow. For others—a process to follow and check on how we're approaching selling the product. Provides multiple approaches to selling a customer. Requires better planning. Prompts retrieval of information useful for proactive approach to problems."

— a salesperson with 15 years experience

"As a new representative (1 year) the Process is a valuable tool. The Process takes a complex and sometimes overwhelming job and gives me a concrete and workable plan. Its flow chart gives me direction and allows me to focus on the various aspects of the job and prioritize my goals. As a result, I feel the process makes me "work smart" as well as work hard! The process also allows me to continually assess and revise my territory plan. In a challenging and dynamic field this continual assessment and revision is a must in order to ensure success. I would recommend the Process For Learning, Sharing, and Selling to all sales representatives."

"I look at the Process as my guideline to help me plan, prioritize, and organize my territory as my "business." It helps me to know where I am with the customer."

— a one-year salesperson.

"The process has helped me organize my thoughts and goals for each customer. Is helpful in establishing strategies and has helped in discovering ways to evaluate results."

— a five-year salesperson.

"The process has been helpful to me by providing a mental 'bookmark' in thinking about what I want to do with the product with a particular customer or group of customers. That is it keeps me from losing my place in my thinking process. Also, I am currently using it to help me identify areas to concentrate on with individual customers. This will eventually become my plan of action for the 1st trimester of [next year]. It has also helped me think about specific areas I wish to concentrate on for my personal development plan for [next year]."

— a salesperson with 20 years experience.

Spread of the Q-Factor

These responses show that the sales force found the new methods overwhelmingly beneficial. The success of the program was backed up by the bottom line numbers, too— further evidence that if you focus on improving the processes, sales results will naturally improve:

- From the July to the June before we instituted the new process, our top product in sales experienced a .7% decrease in total dollars and held a 47.4 share of market.
- From the June when we began until the following December, we saw a 14.7% increase in total dollars and increased our market-share to 52.0%.
- By December of the next year, we saw another 12.8% increase in total dollars and rose to a 54.2% share of the market.

Let me make one thing clear—and hopefully this is obvious to all readers—it is not the process that sells. Salespeople sell! They are the only reason that we were able to turn our top product around and get it back on a growth curve in a market that included 16 major competitors. The salespeople deserve all of the credit and recognition for this outstanding, exceptional performance. Any process is only as good as the salespeople's commitment, enthusiasm, and abilities. I'm blessed to have worked with such an outstanding group of people.

6

PART SIX

Instilling Trust

One of a manager's most important jobs is building an environment based on trust. By trust I mean something more than the old concept of loyalty, which means being faithful and steadfast. Loyalty in the workplace implied a one-way relationship, an unconditional, blind attachment, and while it was an honorable quality, the concept is being replaced. The relationship between employer and employee is now defined by a more straightforward word, commitment. "Commitment" refers to the act of pledging oneself or being emotionally bound to a specific course of action. Commitment is a two-way, often contractual agreement that is built on mutual benefit. It is important for managers to understand this distinction in order to spare everyone the confusion that can result from trying to adhere to poorly understood and outdated concepts.

"Self-trust is the first secret of success."
— *Ralph Waldo Emerson*

"Self-confidence is the first great requisite to great undertakings."
— *Samuel Johnson*

"Let every man's hope be in himself." —Virgil

Building trust is something else again, and as always seems to be the case, the work begins with ourselves. Trust means firm reliance on the integrity, ability, or character of a person or thing. Managers must first establish trust in themselves, their beliefs, and their intuitions, before they can change the way others think about themselves and their work. Trust is earned. Once you are confident that what you are doing is correct and valuable, you can act with a conviction and consistency that will instill confidence and trust among the people around you.

A group of salespeople recently identified nine actions that build trust. The list that they constructed is most revealing:

Trust-Building Actions

- Communicate/provide feedback on agreed-to objectives
- Share "what to do" and "how to's."
- Candid and open communication with objectives, goals, strategies and expectations of each other.
- Sharing and accepting each other's strengths to help achieve goals.
- Spending adequate time together to work and get to know one another.
- Keeping personal information confidential.
- Understanding the performance evaluation and compensation systems.
- Sharing responsibility for goals, strategies and evaluating progress.
- Creating a safe, caring work environment that encourages:
    risk taking
    room for error/broad boundaries
    rewarding failure
    recognition
    forgiveness
    positive feedback

Openness in communication is essential to establishing trust. Of course, certain information is privileged to management and should not be recklessly disseminated. But this is not a severely limiting consideration. If questions or concerns about privileged topics come up when you are talking to members of your team, be up front about being unable to share that information. Never attempt to hide or twist things around out of fear that telling it straight will make you or your company look bad. Bad news is never easy to give, but hiding it or trying to put a positive spin on it only makes matters worse. Anything that might be interpreted as deceptive communication leads to a feeling of mistrust, and this is not only detrimental to immediate job performance but also breaks down the bonds which can be so important within your work group. When a salesperson feels that his or her manager can be trusted, on the other hand, then even when there are difficulties, the atmosphere can be one of working together to make it through.

The same group of salespeople also identified seven actions that build openness in communications:

Open-Communication Actions

- Initiating communication, listening, and considering the feedback.
- Opening the boundaries of our territories to include others without losing the connections and relationships that build synergy.
- Sharing information, insight, viewpoints, and interpretations that can be beneficial to business.
- Expressing confidence in team members to achieve common goals.
- Welcoming ideas and interactions of others.
- Asking for advice, viewpoints and feedback.
- Being accessible, available, and receptive to new ideas.

A misunderstanding about money issues is a sure way to. damage trust. Every effort should be made to inform, train, and communicate with salespeople about a company's compensation program. Offering overly-optimistic figures up front may boost spirit in the short term, but if these figures don't work out, the end result is negativity and bitterness. Everyone should know the salary ranges of positions and job bands. Bonus and incentive programs should be explained honestly and in detail, pointing out not only the best case scenario but the worst case as well.

An essential aspect of fostering trust is to never reveal confidential information about one person to another. Condoning and participating in negative rumormongering is certain to damage your group's spirit.

People spread rumors for several reasons. Speculating about unpleasant topics is a way to vent anxiety. Complaining or spreading dirt about someone else's qualifications or performance helps reassure some people that they are doing a good job. Rumors, in other words, act as a release valve for legitimate pressures and concerns.

Rumors have several damaging side effects. While gossiping with another person might make it seem that the two of you are establishing a bond by sharing one another's confidence, if that person hears you say something that they know or later find out to be inaccurate, or if they hear you talking about someone they know and like, the end result is not increased confidence but damaged trust. Rumor swapping, furthermore, encourages people to focus on the negative and to miss out on possibilities for recognizing strengths and capitalizing on advantages. A good manager will avoid rumors and attempt to dispel them.

Sales managers can also build trust by the way they conduct job performance reviews. Salespeople should be kept well-informed of how they are doing throughout the year so that there are no surprises for them at their performance review. Although it is easier to ignore little problems with the hope that they will go away, these little problems often snowball into bigger problems. If you have created a relationship of trust with the salespeople, they will understand that you are not being picky or harping on trivial things when you point out small difficulties. They will understand that you are trying to work with them to ensure overall quality and improvement.

Trust is always a crucial element of your relationship with the coworkers; but in times of career uncertainty, it becomes essential. If conditions are difficult, knowing that their team members respect them and are honest with them offers personal support and will help smooth out the bumps.

Part of that honesty is making sure that you and those around you keep an eye on the future. Look beyond your current job. Build on strengths, knowledge, skills, and experience that your present company will need in the future. Look for opportunities for improvement in activities and projects that are results-oriented and can help develop these valuable commodities. Create and keep updated a file of your achievements, innovations, and experiences for your resume.

Prioritize the career opportunities you would want if you were to change jobs. Learn about these jobs—what education, skills, knowledge, and experience they require. Then network and learn from top people in those fields what they will require in the near future. Network, network, and network again. But above all, know that you are already perfect and have everything you need.

As Katherine Hepburn said, "The secret of a happy life is not having everything you want, it's wanting everything you have."

This futuristic attitude and atmosphere of trust can help dissolve the anxiety that so easily develops in today's less certain workplace. How many people would need to benefit in order for the effort to be worthwhile? In my opinion, just one. What do you think?

7

PART SEVEN

Rules of the Road for the Sales Professional

A sales representative's workplace is typically someone else's office. He or she may deal with a different set of people in a different locality each day. Transportation—whether by plane, auto, or both—has built-in aggravations and delays. Obtaining food and shelter of a predictable and acceptable quality brings its own set of challenges, and after making it to the client's office, the rep still has to get past the secretary. Finally, between brief periods of camaraderie enjoyed at training sessions or sales meetings, the sales rep must maintain a sense of team spirit and stay focused on corporate goals even though his or her closest coworker may be half-a-state away.

Somehow, the best sales representatives not only conquer these obstacles but thrive on the stimulus they provide. Occasionally you see sales reps who move through the daily round of offices, hotels and restaurants with ease and assurance, knowing that they are truly welcome wherever they go. When I notice someone like that, an individual who enjoys the job and does it superlatively, I think to myself, "Here is someone who really knows the Rules of the Road!"

There is a great similarity in the way the best and most successful salespeople handle themselves in the field. Successful salespeople do things that work, things that bring out their personal best and elicit a genuinely positive response from others. They operate on a system of Do's and Don'ts that smooth difficult pathways and make the daily human interchange a lot easier. These "Rules of the Road" (as I have always thought of them) can be hard to pin down, but the best salespeople follow them as carefully as a diplomat observes the rules of protocol.

Some things change. The top salesperson today may look like, dress like, and be the product of M.I.T. or Harvard Business School. His or her territory may be the Far East or the eastern United States. But the Rules remain the same. We've just evolved a few new ones to meet current needs.

Here are the "Rules of the Road" as I know them, a practical handbook for the man or woman on the road. I offer it along with the following observation: Today, as always, the player with the best grasp of the rules has the best chance to win the game.

Rules of the Road for the Sales Professional

1. Believe in yourself, your products, and your company.
2. Keep your word.
3. Write out a vision statement for yourself.
4. Don't use lack of time, money, or personnel as an excuse.
5. Be considerate of your customer's time.
6. Avoid pessimism and sarcasm.
7. Make time for your family, first.
8. Then remember, business before pleasure.
9. Send your reports in on time.
10. Learn what it is you need to know.
11. Develop excellent manners.
12. Use the sales aids.
13. Learn to plan a great presentation.
14. Keep your car clean and waxed.
15. Get independent.
16. Make the customer feel special.
17. Nothing is as easy as it looks.

18. Everything takes longer than it ought to.
19. Don't get mad when life keeps proving #17 and #18 to you.
20. Do more than you have to do.
21. Learn when and how to motivate yourself.
22. Be the first to move toward the other person.
23. Enjoy the expense account: Tip doormen, bellmen, and maids.
24. Stay at hotels that have valet parking.
25. Do it now.
26. Go out with your spouse every Friday or Saturday night, especially when you don't really want to.
27. Treat your spouse as you would your best customer.
28. Think, think, and think.
29. Have a desk and office area for work at home.
30. Find out when and where you are when most creative.
31. Read, read, and read.
32. Manage your money.
33. Get a haircut if you think you need one.
34. Don't bite your fingernails.
35. Always be polite to service people.
36. Don't expect so much, so quickly.
37. You can listen, but don't tell off-colored jokes.
38. Learn to smile easily.
39. Learn to laugh and do it often.
40. Eat at the best restaurants when with customers.
41. Take a public speaking course.
42. Never promise more than you can deliver.
43. Be sincere and believable.
44. Learn to celebrate; then plan it and do it.
45. Read a book on how to dress successfully.
46. Help your boss.
47. Dress as well as your best customer.
48. Be courteous to all salespeople.

49.   Watch your language.

50.   Learn how the compensation system works.

51.   Never knock the competition. Learn from them.

52.   Go first class.

53.   Be five minutes early.

54.   Learn your best colors and review them before shopping.

55.   Listen, listen, and listen.

56.   Figure out what motivates you, besides money.

57.   Help some new people get into the business.

58.   Picture your customer doing what you want.

59.   Don't be so hard on yourself.

60.   Don't drive a car that's more expensive than your best customer's.

61.   Choose a car that reflects your good sense of values.

62.   Give some of your time to someone who cannot do anything for your business.

63.   Watch your breath.

64.   Treat all customers like your best customer.

65.   Learn the advantages and disadvantages of your product compared to competitive ones.

66.   Spend time learning from your customer.

67.   Be careful whom you qualify as the best potential customer.

68.   Call on older customers and others who cannot use or buy as much as they used to.

69.   Call on new or younger customers who cannot use or buy a lot yet.

70.   Never let anyone put a bumper sticker on your car.

71.   Get to know your airline's Special Services Representative.

72.   Be careful whose name you use as a reference or proof.

73.   Above all, your credibility is your most important asset.

74.   Learn to use word pictures in your presentation.

75.   Offer to be there for any new person.

76.   Know what you want, what you need, and learn to tell the difference.

77. Know what your customer wants and needs, but let him or her distinguish between the two.
78. Ask for what you want.
79. Remember the wisdom of Dennis Waitley: "You get what you need by giving others what they want."
80. Enjoy nature.
81. Don't gossip.
82. Say only what you want to hear repeated.
83. Follow up, follow up, and follow up.
84. Enjoy the present.
85. Keep memories safe.
86. Learn from your failures.
87. Reward your failures.
88. Take risks.
89. Believe in yourself and others.
90. Believe in miracles.
91. Plan your work. Work your plan.
92. Forgive yourself and others.
93. Say your prayers.
94. Show respect for everybody.
95. Learn the names of everyone working in your customer's office. Take time for them.
96. Don't use the "dumb country boy" approach. Don't manipulate.
97. Don't use the "dumb blonde" approach. Don't manipulate.
98. Trust others and yourself.
99. Make the best use of your time.
100. Take the time to relax, slow down, and smell the roses.
101. Visit a cemetery.
102. Go to a friend's funeral.
103. Don't take yourself or life so seriously.
104. Initiate, initiate, and initiate.
105. Carry a hundred dollar bill in your wallet or purse.

106. Get up early and get out amongst them.
107. Don't quit on a bad call.
108. Make an extra call.
109. Do what you are supposed to do.
110. Learn about the customer.
111. Remember: Emotions are why people buy, not facts and not information.
112. So learn your customer's emotional needs.
113. Accept the credit and the blame.
114. Provide the little special touches.
115. Learn something about the area or town before you try to sell.
116. Get a shoe shine or manicure.
117. Serve the customer.
118. Earn the right to close.
119. Entertain yourself.
120. Entertain others.
121. Focus on results.
122. Don't criticize or try to reform.
123. Read your mail every day.
124. Listen to the customer's interests.
125. Help the other salespeople in your company.
126. Be proud of yourself, your products, and your company.
127. Find out for yourself.
128. Compete with yourself, not others.
129. Always extend a helping hand.
130. Establish your own values, but respect the values of others.
131. Listen to your voice mail every day.
132. Remember your priorities.
133. Learn to laugh at yourself.
134. Remember there are three sides to every story: yours, mine, and the truth.
135. Don't walk in on competitors. Wait your turn.

136.   Call on everybody.
137.   Entertain new ideas.
138.   Monitor and chart progress.
139.   Share what you think.
140.   Learn from others.
141.   Single out the best to become friends with.
142.   Decide what you will and will not do.
143.   Save the company some money.
144.   Determine what a good job is.
145.   Put your best foot forward.
146.   Show your emotions. Be happy.
147.   Have a firm handshake.
148.   Look for the positive.
149.   Be generous.
150.   Develop a good memory for names and details and needs.
151.   Exercise, eat right, and stay slim.
152.   If you choose to drink, do it like a lady or a gentleman.
153.   Don't smoke. It's out-of-date.
154.   Work at your relationships.
155.   Nothing stays the same: It increases or declines.
156.   Sometimes you don't have a problem to solve, you have a decision to make.
157.   Establish goals and objectives.
158.   Look at all of your assets.
159.   Concentrate on doing a fine job where you are.
160.   Build on your strengths.
161.   Learn the social amenities.
162.   Play golf and tennis.
163.   Take a position.
164.   Watch how you spend money: It's better to be tight than to be a show-off.
165.   Be candid and forthright with your customer.
166.   Don't use fear as a motivator.
167.   Decide how to make the customer a hero.

168. Give the customer your best presentation.
169. Remember other people's needs, interests, and goals.
170. Don't apologize for taking your customer's time. Make your visit worth his while.
171. Excuse yourself before you get smashed.
172. Pay attention to get to know everybody.
173. Encourage yourself and everyone else to become the best they can.
174. Forget the competition.
175. Celebrate progress.
176. Learn to love others and to forgive.
177. Put up with an unbearable boss. You are learning something and nothing lasts forever.
178. Don't let a bad boss mess up a good job.
179. Dream big dreams. Choose dreams over goals.
180. Learn to love your job and your company.
181. Learn how to cook for others.
182. Send thank-you notes.
183. Listen to anybody about a better job.
184. Change your shirt or blouse at night before dinner.
185. Serve your family.
186. Organize your car trunk like you would your office.
187. Become an expert at something.
188. Write a letter to your customers who retire.
189. File only what's necessary.
190. Prioritize: Must do, should do, and want to do.
191. Watch out for being too slick.
192. Don't use profanity.
193. Never argue with a customer.
194. Be a good team player.
195. Learn how to rest when traveling.
196. Go to the movies.
197. Pack enough clothes for your different business functions.

198. Be ambitious to do a good job at your job.

199. Prepare yourself to do a good job at your job.

200. Have fun at your job.

201. Drive safely and courteously.

202. Take time for a coffee or cola break.

203. Learn to think about others.

204. Choose hotels with exercise equipment and use it.

205. See medical and dental checkups as required maintenance for the body.

206. Keep a positive outlook.

207. Be prepared.

208. Create win-win situations.

209. Don't talk business during meals.

210. Develop a tradition.

211. Find out who the local influentials are. Get to know them and learn from them.

212. Establish goals, determine useful checkpoints, and celebrate progress.

213. Learn how to set up an office.

214. Be patient.

215. Be around fun and positive people.

216. Be kind.

217. Tip 15% for any level of service—not all of your calls will be good—and tip 20% for good service.

218. Don't carry your own bags in a hotel.

219. Don't write a letter in anger. Wait at least 24 hours.

220. Tell your wife or husband that they are your best friend.

221. Accept, admire, and appreciate others.

222. Learn to enjoy your own company.

223. Know whether your customer likes facts and details, or just the broad strokes.

224. Assume responsibility for making the most of your job.

225. Learn how to elevate your performance.

226. Keep a file on your accomplishments.

227. Write out your presentation.
228. Discipline, discipline, and discipline.
229. Walk at a brisk pace.
230. Park in the shade with the window down.
231. Find a convenient place for telephone calls.
232. Walk up the stairs.
233. Have a nice suitcase.
234. Stay in, have room service, and relax.
235. Listen to audio tapes in your car.
236. Establish your spiritual, personal, family, and business goals.
237. Keep a "Month-at-a-Glance" calendar.
238. Use a Daytimer, Franklin, or some other daily planner.
239. Buy and use a nice fountain pen.
240. Carry your yellow legal pad in a nice leather holder.
241. Organize your briefcase.
242. Enlarge your perception of your job.
243. Help a new salesperson.
244. Don't date anyone in the customer's office. (If you can, the boss probably already has.)
245. Take the time to make yourself feel special.
246. Look for the right things to do, then worry how to do them the right way.
247. Don't put your pen in the company's inkwell.
248. Learn how to hug.
249. Don't appear to be using your sexuality.
250. Look good, act good, and be good.
251. Be interested in your customers.
252. Keep helpful customer records.
253. Don't write down anything you wouldn't want your customer to see.
254. Pre-plan your objective for each call.
255. Evaluate your calls and performance by results—not activity and how hard you think you work.
256. Work smarter, not harder.

257. Study sales skills. You still don't use them all.
258. Become an expert in certain sales skills and be able to teach them to others.
259. Exercise your sales skills until they become second nature to you.
260. Run your territory as if it were your own business.
261. Take a customer to lunch each week. Be frugal.
262. Do expense reports accurately and on time.
263. Develop high standards for yourself.
264. Don't read to or appear to teach your customers.
265. Remember the 20%-80% rule, but see everybody in your territory.
266. Ask your boss to work in the field with you.
267. After you say, "I don't know," find out.
268. Develop your curiosity.
269. Don't follow all company plans.
270. Assume the responsibility to learn the most effective sales approaches.
271. Share your ideas.
272. Don't use a customer's name until you have his/her permission.
273. Do it first.
274. Determine the key message you want your customer to remember.
275. Keep a journal.
276. Keep good company after work.
277. Stay in top hotels.
278. Learn impeccable table manners and use them.
279. Be able to read a fancy menu.
280. Know how to order wine.
281. Eat in the top restaurants but also know the best meat-and-three-vegetables places.
282. Be pleasant to waiters and waitresses.
283. Realize that we are all God's children.

284. Be excited and enthusiastic.
285. Don't take rejection personally.
286. Sell as much as possible of a new product. The more you sell now, the more you will continue to sell.
287. Be willing to concede the obviously superior qualities of a competitive product.
288. Give up all grievances.
289. Never prove the customer to be wrong.
290. Manage your time, your resources, and your money.
291. Acquire a small group of peers who will level with you.
292. Use a conversational approach to selling.
293. Realize that you are worth a lot more than your job.
294. Keep building self-confidence.
295. Learn to see four opportunities for every one problem in a situation.
296. What you give out you will get back.
297. Listen to the negatives about your product.
298. Distinguish between a real complaint and a customer's attempt to make conversation.
299. Be flexible.
300. Let your good customers know how important they are to you and the company.
301. Let your boss know you respect him. Even if he or she is a jerk, there's something you can respect and learn from that person.
302. Take two weeks vacation at one time.
303. Call as soon as you know that you are going to be late for an appointment.
304. Get a car phone even if you don't think you need one.
305. Equip your office.
306. Take time to goof off.
307. Daydream.
308. Don't waste your resources.
309. Learn how to rejuvenate your energies.

310. Choose friends and associates who are smarter than you.

311. Learn how to leave work at work.

312. Take the time to play.

313. If you don't like the beach or shore, go anyway. You will learn to value water touching sand, and it will become an important resource for you.

314. Welcome objections to your product.

315. Learn to love.

316. Wear a very good watch, but make sure it's classic and not flashy.

317. Forgive somebody.

318. Remember that your spouse is your best and most important friend. Act accordingly.

319. Go to work when you don't feel like it.

320. Keep it simple.

321. Pump your own gas.

322. Why hang onto your hostilities?

223. Have a consistent savings plan and save at least 15% of your net pay.

324. Find out about tithing.

325. Give something away.

326. Remember and believe: what goes around comes around.

327. Develop a profile guide for learning about your customer. Use it.

328. Send loving thoughts to others.

329. Learn who your resources are. Go to the right person for candor, advice, support, love, or encouragement.

330. Don't give advice unless asked. You will not be asked very often.

331. Communicate with your boss.

332. Learn how to negotiate with your customer.

333. Become a successful businessperson.

334. Take a course.

335. Watch a videotape on salesmanship.
336. Do a preceptorship.
337. Learn, learn, and learn.
338. Remember, asking people you have just met where they live and what they do is like asking them their credentials. It's rude.
339. Go for a walk.
340. Beware of becoming judgmental.
341. Don't step on a bug.
342. Send your children to public school.
343. Be inclusive.
344. Don't discuss money with others.
345. Don't sue anybody unless you absolutely have to.
346. Participate in every learning/incentive program your company offers.
347. Don't judge a sales program or sales tool until you have tried it at least twelve times.
348. Take good care of company equipment.
349. Accept new challenges and give it your best.
350. Look for new business opportunities.
351. Read a biography of someone you admire.
352. Find someone to admire.
353. Don't job hop.
354. Build a track record.
355. Know your strengths and skills.
356. Figure out your purpose in life.
357. Become open-minded.
358. Remember judgment of others is one of your worst enemies.
359. Be optimistic.
360. Stay healthy in mind, body, and spirit.
361. Don't drive while feeling hostile.
362. Understand that big discrepancies between expectation and reality cause stress.

363. All of your needs have already been met.
364. You can't avoid stress and anxiety, so learn how to handle it.
365. Do your own yard work and wash your own car.
366. Keep a file folder on your very top customers. Drop in ideas you have for them and clippings that you know will interest them.
367. Make a list of special things that you can do for a particular customer: an information video, a small plant for a new office, etc.
368. Establish an open-door policy for your territory.
369. See your customers on a regular basis.
370. Have an itinerary for each month.
371. See customers based on their interests and yours.
372. Figure out what will make you happy and go for it.
373. Don't try to get all of the business.
374. Show the similarities of your product to the one they are using.
375. Differentiate your products and yourself from competitors.
376. Don't fall for the trap of making calls just so you can report them.
377. Know what to say if a customer tells you they're too busy, and suggests you put them down for a call anyway.
378. Do not cheat on your call activities report.
379. Don't cheat.
380. Let anybody you know come in your back door at home.
381. Remember the sale is not closed until the customer is satisfied.
382. Marketing 101 is knowing your product's benefits in order of importance. Find out the customer's order of importance.
383. Learn several different ways to expand the usage of your product.

384. Remember the pathway: Awareness, knowledge, trial user, user, and supporter of your products. Know where each customer is on the path.

385. Don't lead people on.

386. Always remember customers are people first.

387. Keep a long-range approach to building business relationships.

388. I will say it again: "Credibility is your most important asset."

389. A salesperson renews his or her contract each year. This comes with the territory.

390. You have all the security you need.

391. Add to mind-sets rather than trying to change them.

392. Since some people judge on appearances, give them a chance to judge you correctly.

393. Enjoy your hobbies. (Get one after you put your family and job first.)

394. Rent a car or take a cab while your car is in the shop.

395. Remember forgiveness is easier to get than approval.

396. Admit when you have been wrong. Look down at your feet, shuffle around, and say you won't do it again. And don't.

397. Commitment is a voluntary decision.

398. I'm willing to repeat it, "Take Risks!"

399. Figure out what you can do to increase your productivity.

400. You have to spend money to make money.

401. Spend your company's money as you would spend your own.

402. To sell, you have to see the right person, with the right product, with the right frequency, with the right message.

403. Don't say, "Trust me." Demonstrate your trustworthiness.

404. If you have to tell people what you have done for them, then you haven't done enough for them.

405. The first person you have to sell to is yourself.

406. You will see it when you believe it.
407. Fair is at the fairgrounds in October.
408. "Life is not fair, but God is good," says Robert Schuller. Read one or several of his books.
409. Remember that it's all in your mind.
410. Search for inner peace, happiness, and wisdom.
411. Realize the power of love and forgiveness.
412. Talk to yourself in positive terms.
413. Self-talk is very helpful!
414. Become an expert in time management.
415. Waste some time, but know when you are doing it and do it on purpose.
416. Accept people at their word until proven otherwise.
417. You are perfect the way you are and you are at the right place in your personal development.
418. Focus on systems or processes.
419. Be able to sell the value of your product whether it is priced high or low.
420. Double-check friendly tips from the competition, not from distrust, but because anyone can be wrong and not know it.
421. Everybody targets the high potential customer: You will have to show credentials, credibility, and service in order to achieve your sales goals.
422. When the customer does not buy, we should assume responsibility for having chosen the wrong prospect, addressed the wrong needs or interests, or made the wrong presentation.
423. When they have bought one product, they will buy the second and third.
424. Communicate your ideas.
425. Develop your persistence.
426. Each day, look for a way to improve your performance. When you find one, try it every day for three weeks.

427. Move from an "I" frame of reference to a "we" frame of reference.

428. Work hard to build a good self-image.

429. It's only when we are trying our best, using our talents, and giving our love to our job that we feel good about ourselves and are building self-esteem.

430. Be open and always make the effort for other people.

431. Keep a positive attitude.

432. Remember that the best thing about a sales career is that it keeps us focused on building relationships based on trust and concern for one another.

433. Never use a sales tool that gives the customer a test.

434. Commit yourself to developing good work habits.

435. Know the key nondecision makers.

436. Your customers appreciate your attentiveness and respect toward the people they work with.

437. Get prepared before meetings and participate.

438. Don't complain about the food and sleeping accommodations at meetings.

439. Remember, it takes a long time to build a solid reputation and you can lose it in one day or night.

440. Be faithful to your wife or husband. Can you trust someone who isn't?

441. When you fail or make big mistakes, learn from them and move on.

442. Live in the present.

443. Carry clippings of motivational and inspirational quotes or sayings with you in your wallet or briefcase.

444. Plan, plan, and plan.

445. Learn to be clear and concise with your communications, written or oral.

446. First get it written. Then get it right.

447. Learn whom to shake hands with, whom to hug, whom to kiss. And under what circumstances.

448. If you know you have a great product, don't let the customer shake your conviction.
449. Make your voice one of your best tools.
450. Tell both sides of the sales story, not to gain believability, but to serve your customer.
451. Don't wait for more ammunition: Go into battle with what you have.
452. Have fun. That, too, is your responsibility.

8

PART EIGHT

Rules of the Road for the Sales Manager

If you're a new manager, you were probably a pretty good salesperson. And if you are a typical new manager, you will probably fit the following profile rather closely:

- You have had at least 3 to 5 years successful selling experience.
- You are having to relocate yourself or yourself and family.
- You are nervous about the change in jobs and locale.
- You have read and learned what your interests are in *The Rules of the Road for the Sales Professional.*
- You already work hard.
- You are ambitious to do a good job as a manager.
- You are not sure what is the next job that you want.
- You are not altogether sure how well you will do as a manager.
- You have been overmanaged and underled.
- You have read several books and listened to several audio-tapes on management.
- You have not yet examined and established your own beliefs about management and leadership.
- You respect your company and feel positive about the future of your industry and the role your company will have in the future.
- You are eager to prepare yourself, but worry that there is not enough time and specific training available for you to learn to do a good job.

The following are instructions, suggestions, advice, and ideas about how to become a successful manager, have fun on the job, and make a difference in the productivity and careers of the people you work with.

Rules of the Road for the Sales Manager

1.   Be at least 70 to 80 per cent sure that you want the job.

2.   Have the real support of your spouse for the job and relocation. Don't settle for "I'm for whatever you want."

3.   Remember your good track record as a salesperson, but forget how you did it. Nobody cares and it's not relevant.

4.   Trust the people you work with.

5.   Assume that they all want to do a good job.

6.   Keep your humility. Don't become too impressed with yourself.

7.   Learn to ask for help from the people you work with...and mean it!

8.   Ask for specific advice from your peers.

9.   Build a friendship with managers that you feel do a good job.

10.   Make an early decision about whose side you will be on: the people you work with or management.

11.   Get to know the people you work with, their perceptions, goals, concerns, interests, etc.

12. Do not, do not refer to them as "your people" or "your troops."

13. They do not work for you. You work together.

14. Be lazy enough to let them do the job.

15. Realize that you are not very important to them. i.e., "Managers are good for helping to push the car out of the snow." "Managers can help you jump-start your car."

16. Don't try to change anybody but yourself.

17. The salespeople already have the knowledge and skills to do a good job.

18. The problem is not how they do their job, but how you look at it.

19. Don't criticize in public or private.

20. Judgment will be one of your worst enemies.

21. Forget the saying "familiarity breeds contempt." You can work with your best friend or relative if you are confident in your relationships and priorities.

22. Learn to love your company, the people you work with, and your job.

23. Be human and remember that the people you work with are people first.

24. Don't be afraid to show your ignorance.

25. You lead best by example when you are not trying to be an example.

26. Don't become a workaholic.

27. Work your hours, not theirs.

28. Don't send out itineraries.

29. Don't take the job if you don't really care about serving the people you work with.

30. Learn to run a good and productive meeting. Learn to be a good moderator. It takes two days to plan each single day of meeting time. Delegate.

31. Be positive.

32. Learn Situational Leadership. (Charles Blanchard)

33. Read *The One-Minute Manager.*

34. Share what you read with the people you work with. Find out what they are reading.

35. Develop your character by examining the values you believe in and practice.

36. Don't set territorial goals and quotas. Have group/team goals.

37. Establish a vision with your team or group.

38. Believe in teamsmanship.

39. Your most important task is to hire top people.

40. Your second most important task is to create an environment of trust and mutual respect for one another.

41. Help applicants to decide whether they want to join your team and company.

42. Once they have been hired, do everything possible to see that they succeed. Don't let them fail.

43. Build a good relationship with your boss: Consult, communicate, ask for his or her help.

44. Don't do the selling for the salespeople. That's their job.

45. Don't let reports get in the way.

46. Strive to create an atmosphere in which the salespeople come to you with their needs.

47. Put a hammer in a man's hand and he will start nailing down everything. Don't problem-solve until you know what the real problem is; then decide whose problem it is.

48. Learn to be a fair administrator, a good manager, an excellent learner, a smart leader, and a caring person.

49. Always pick up the tab when you are with the salespeople.

50. Remember the salespeople. The people you work with are your best customers.

51. Value the differences in the people you work with.

52. Build on their strengths. It's only rare that you have to deal with weaknesses, so you can overcompensate with strengths and leave most weaknesses alone. (Besides, who's to say they are really weaknesses?)

53. Give the benefit of any doubt to the salespeople.

54. Learn to selectively listen to your management— they will drive you nuts if you do everything they tell you to do.

55. Focus on what the salesperson wants.

56. Concentrate on ethics and values—then learning— then results—then skills—then activities.

57. Encourage goal-setting by the salespeople.

58. Set a good example with planning and goal-setting with the team.

59. Be sincerely interested in your personal development.

60. Share yourself.

61. Celebrate progress.

62. Learn the motivational levers that you command, and above all, praise, praise, praise.

63. Don't be afraid to reprimand, just be hesitant. Make sure you have the facts.

64. Make sure everybody knows the right things to do (what) and, if necessary, how to do things the right way (how).

65. Work with consensus. You don't have time for everybody to agree.

66. Keep or develop your sense of humor. It really helps a group to relax and to enjoy each other.

67. Be patient with your family about relocating. Listen, listen, listen, and do not use the "Yes, but..." approach.

68. Buy a better house than you can afford. Your income will go up.

69. Keep your family ahead of your career in priority.

70. Follow the "earned-right" principle.

71. Establish clearly, in writing, what you can do to help the salespeople achieve their goals. Let them decide what help or assistance they want and when.

72. Do no harm. First, stay out of the way.

73. Learn alongside the people you work with about the customer's expectations, values, goals, needs, perceptions, and interests.

74. Practice M.B.W.A. or M.B.S.A.: management by wandering or standing around. It's more learning than management.

75.   Remember that the salesperson is the boss in his or her territory.

76.   Learn to enjoy making customer calls with the salesperson, but don't sell and don't push yourself in. The major objective is for the customer to be sold, not for you to see the customer.

77.   If the customer asks whether you are there to check up on the salesperson, your answer is "Absolutely not. I'm here to learn why they do so well." You are not there to judge. You are there to learn from the customer.

78.   You may have a fine, fancy office or you may have a room in the basement. It doesn't make any difference because your real office is with the salespeople.

79.   Your most important time with the salespeople is spent listening to them and to the customers.

80.   If the customer asks you an important question, turn to the salesperson for the answer.

81.   Do everything you can to build up the salesperson in the eyes of the customer.

82.   You are there at the invitation of the salesperson.

83.   The salesperson is the authority or expert on the products and company.

84.   If the setting is not convenient for the salesperson, customer and you, i.e., only two chairs, excuse yourself and thank the customer for their help.

85.   If it appears that you and the salesperson will have a hard time seeing the customer, let the receptionist know that it's not necessary for both of you to see the customer and that the salesperson, alone, can get in and out quicker. This supports the salesperson and helps get in more calls.

86.   If after several calls, the salesperson is really making a mistake in his/her presentations (facts, not judgment), then get to the right place and right time to discuss it. The right place and time is not driving 70 m.p.h. on the Interstate.

87.   Don't talk about so many subjects, especially while driving.

88.   Offer to drive when it would be convenient for the other person.

89.   Plan your visits/trips the way you want them to plan their calls.

90.   What are the objectives of the visit together, theirs and yours? Have these been communicated? How and when can the objectives best be accomplished? If there are too many objectives, complete theirs first.

91.   Don't try to train when the salesperson does not want to learn. You are wasting your time and confusing or frustrating the salesperson.

92.   You can't teach until the student shows up.

93.   A teacher will appear when you really want to learn.

94.   We are all teachers to one another.

95.   You teach what you need. The best way to learn is to teach.

96. You see what you think. See the best in everybody you work with.

97. You'll see it when you believe it. (Wayne Dyer).

98. Don't gossip.

99. Honor the chain of command.

100. Your clients are the people you work with, your boss and home office staff, and your peers.

101. Give the credit to the individuals and team and accept the blame by yourself.

102. The best things to learn and teach are skills because they can be used each day and improved upon.

103. Reinforce everything you see the salespeople doing well.

104. Set a good example with people in all walks of life. Demonstrate respect.

105. Take a break and just chat with one another.

106. Be on time...or 5 minutes early.

107. Remember that new people have a lot to learn. Don't encourage them to call customers by their first name.

108. Show new salespeople how to pack a briefcase and trunk.

109. Don't consider anything too small or too basic to discuss.

110. Help them to set up an office and teach them what to keep and what to throw away. Do this even with very experienced people.

111. Stop what you are doing any time that a person calls about a job and asks for your help.

112. The best new employees will be recommended by your present workforce. Interview everyone they recommend.

113. Treat the salespeople to a fine lunch and take them out with their spouses to a fine dinner at least once a year.

114. When out of town, know how to stop work at the end of the day and go to a movie.

115. Learn how to entertain yourself with new ideas and other people.

116. Find out what the salespeople need and try to get it for them.

117. If you want them to sell to their customers' needs and wants, then try to satisfy theirs.

118. Take two weeks vacation during the summer.

119. Try to give your families what they want on weekends.

120. Be financially responsible. Manage your money well and encourage the salespeople to save each month.

121. Visit a good book store each month and browse the business section for new books and ideas.

122. Dress well and expect the salespeople to do the same.

123. Be open and candid about the compensation system.

124. Don't over-reward poor or average performance. Remember that you get what you measure and reward.

125. You can't pay a consistently top performer too much. He or she should earn more than the manager.

126. Stay on top of the sales figures. Look for the good news.

127. Be sure to thank the customer's secretary/receptionist when you leave.

128. Take advantage of every opportunity to thank somebody.

129. Learn to send flowers before the funeral.

130. Learn to say "I appreciate you," "You are great," "I'm lucky to work with you..."

131. Integrity is your greatest strength.

132. Spend most of your time with new people, but be there for everybody.

133. Write notes often to praise and to thank the people you work with.

134. Develop and share the skill of visualization: the ability to see the end result of what you want to achieve.

135. Encourage the people you work with to form their own vision of what they want to become and do.

136. Read and share *The One-Minute Salesperson.*

137. Read and study about any subject that is of interest to you and potentially helpful to your work group and business.

138. Stay open-minded. If you are not now, get to be soon because you will need the ideas and flexibility to do well, at best, and to survive, at the worst.

139. Hire people of different ethnic, religious, cultural and educational backgrounds because all kinds of people want to do well and you will learn more from their varied insights.

140. Everybody is entitled to miracles and miracles come in all sizes.

141. Demonstrate respect for everybody you come in contact with and those you don't see.

142. Don't learn or teach manipulative sales techniques.

143. You can improve relationships by increasing communication, trust, affection, or mutual interests.

144. Don't use four-letter words. They just show a poor vocabulary.

145. Don't treat the women you work with the same as the men. They are different—but then, we are all different.

146. Recognize and praise initiative whenever you see it. This characteristic will be high on the list of why you and your group will be successful.

147. Teach everybody to do their paperwork accurately and on time.

148. Communicate the bad news to your boss early.

149. Do more than is expected and don't promise more than you can deliver.

150. Be responsible—respond with ability.

151. Give the people you work with the small, special touches that show you care.

152. Don't blame salespeople. Look for the opportunities and problems that can be solved.

153. Hire and develop character and principle-based people.

154. Meet everybody halfway.

155. Make mistakes. Learn from them and admit to them early.

156. Nothing is shared that is withheld and later revealed.

157. Catch up on your paperwork, written communication, and reading when you are out of town.

158. Take your spouse out to dinner every Friday night. Don't come home from meetings all worn out and dragging.

159. Act a certain way and you will become that way.

160. Join Toastmasters and become a clear, concise communicator.

161. Don't be sarcastic.

162. Be committed to excellence, high standards, and continuing improvement...all of which equals quality.

163. Be honest.

164. Learn to hug.

165. Add to your wardrobe at least two seasons each year. Clothes and accessories are a necessary investment.

166. Dress appropriately for specific occasions.

167. When you praise or even reprimand salespeople, touch them and let them know how you feel.

168. Donate to charity or give away any clothes in your closet that you have not used in two years.

169. Eat healthy, stay in shape, exercise, and control the stress.

170. Watch your drinking. You will drink more if you are not checking yourself.

171. Have fun. Encourage others to have fun. Learn how to have fun on the job.

172. Do something special for your spouse's birthday and your anniversary. Show your appreciation for their support of your career.

173. Encourage salespeople to talk to anyone who shows an interest in hiring them...and do the same thing yourself.

174. Avoid negativism.

175. Find comfortable spots where you can conduct business in restaurants and hotels.

176. Do not allow an office in your home to infringe on your family's privacy.

177. Learn to close the office door and keep it closed on weekends.

178. Locate and utilize a good secretarial service. They are around.

179. Learn to dictate using a small tape recorder.

180. Buy a book on how to organize and set up an office.

181. Try all the new gimmicks that can help with time management and administrative duties.

182. Don't wait, beg, bargain, or try to buy your spouse's help in the office.

183. Have a rocking chair in your office, preferably by a window.

184. Put pictures on the walls, not maps.

185. Have a special getaway place in your home for thinking and daydreaming.

186. Don't compete with anyone but your own potential.

187. Share yourself with others.

188. Encourage people to go into sales work.

189. Remember that the salespeople have the best jobs and serve them.

190. Nag the people you work with to participate in any savings program, life insurance options, employee assistance programs, continuing education, and matched contribution programs that are available.

191. Work toward becoming a well-balanced business person and encourage others to do the same.

192. Demonstrate a commitment to trying to improve the world around you by first improving your ability to share the love within you.

193. Learn to manage your money well and spend your company's money as if you ran your own business.

194. Stealing from a big corporation is the same as stealing from a little old lady.

195. Choose the people you will work with very carefully and make available all resources that can help them to decide to join you and your company.

196. Make the time to do nice things for the people you work with.

197. Stay in touch with old friends and make new ones.

198. Build your own library and resources for self-development and share them.

199. Make a commitment to continuing self-improvement and share what you are working on with the people you work with. Ask for their help.

200. Know how to manage your time so that you have time for yourself and your family and friends.

201. Send out loving thoughts. You will get back what you send out.

202. If you don't like what you are getting, look closely at what you are giving.

203. Develop a wide range of interests so that you can broaden your conversation.

204. Learn a new word once a week.

205. Improve your written communication skills.

206. Demonstrate affection and trust in the people you work with and others.

207. A manager's worst enemy is the need for control and feeling important.

208. Send the special people in your life flowers, cards, or notes on big occasions.

209. Don't order a drink, wine, or beer at lunch during the work week.

210. Enjoy nature.

211. Learn to order wine and read a fancy menu. Let others order the wine after you know how.

212. Demonstrate practical safety tips while traveling.

213. Read the local newspapers and learn something about the community you are traveling in.

214. Listen, listen, listen.

215. Teach safety while traveling to the women you work with.

216. On the first interview, if at all possible, talk with the applicant in public places such as a quiet corner in a nice hotel lobby or restaurant.

217.   Learn about the families of the people you work with.

218.   Learn and practice everyday etiquette.

219.   Discuss politics, religion, or anything else without arguing.

220.   Present the best appearance you can but remember it's your spirit that counts.

221.   Buy the best quality of clothes you can afford, but buy them on sale.

222.   Have your teeth cleaned every 6 months.

223.   Have a complete physical exam yearly.

224.   When salespeople are telling you about a success of theirs, don't tell them about someone else's. Listen, listen.

225.   Decide which is more effective: selling or learning.

226.   Don't have any goals without a plan to achieve them.

227.   Fear of losing your job is a good motivator, but not the best.

228.   If you are looking for a creative solution to a problem, list 25 possible answers and the most creative ones will be among the last ones.

229.   Don't work for money, work for the opportunity to serve and learn.

230.   Plan for the worst and hope for the best.

231.   Send your work in on time and expect the same from others. If some don't, beware of reinforcing negative behavior. Simply work to help them and ask them to help you.

232.   Spend some special time with the people you are dependent on.

233. For critical issues, have some contingency plans in place for the strategies that do not work.

234. Concentrate on strategies, not on goals.

235. Set up incentive programs in which everybody has a fair chance to win.

236. Establish team goals and specific strategies where everyone can be recognized and rewarded.

237. Make sure everyone knows how to measure individual contributions.

238. Don't force-rank everybody in a small group according to a bell curve. This is very demoralizing to ones in the middle, which is where most people will be forced.

239. If you must rank, force-rank groups, not individuals.

240. Ranking can and will cause competition between people, whereas what is needed is teamwork.

241. Too many people in business apply sports analogies to teamwork. Sports are not the same as business.

242. Competition and judgment within our own business are two of our worst enemies.

243. For all the good that most job performance reviews cause, we would be better off without them.

244. "Everybody wants to know where they stand." Do they really? Or do they want to know where they are going, what's necessary to get there, and what the rewards are for progress?

245. Try drinking water and fruit juices for meals one day a week and see if you feel better and also have more self-control.

246. Eat properly, drink moderately, if at all, exercise, and be positive and supportive.

247. Celebrate progress and achievement. Of the two, progress is the most important.

248. Become devoted to your job and then it will become your devotion.

249. Remember: "Sticks and stones may break your bones..." but other people's words and opinions cannot harm you.

250. Learn to enjoy traveling. It's not what it's cracked up to be, but it can be refreshing and helpful to your relationships.

251. Our purpose in life is to become the best person we can, and a manager's job is to assist this process first within himself and then to assist the people he works with.

252. Don't waste your time with people who already feel that they have all the answers. They are unteachable. Just lead and manage them.

253. Most of us are overmanaged and underled.

254. A leader's responsibility is to create a shared vision.

255. Learning and teaching is asking the right questions, and part of selling is knowing to ask the questions that you already know the answers to.

256. Demonstrate and encourage more learning than selling and your group will produce more of the results you want.

257. The nice thing about a vision is that it helps to maintain a long-range approach to building relationships rather than cutting the customers and salespeople short by focusing on short-term results.

258. When your group shares a vision, meet with your group to establish a clear set of values and guiding principles.

259. Values and principles help to build on our strengths of character, which then enhances our self-esteem and self-worth.

260. If we are not anchored in firm self-worth, it's difficult to be a real team player.

261. A team player can tell his boss what he really thinks, even when the boss does not want to hear it...and most don't.

262. Positive thoughts about ourselves, others, and what needs to be done are so much more motivating than confrontations and problem solving.

263. The scientific method of learning: confrontation, search, try-out, and evaluation is a great process for development (See *Teacher/Manager Systems* by Irvine H. Millgate.)

264. Think process, process, process, or system, system, system for getting something done, or for continuing improvement, or for moving toward your vision. (Millgate)

265. Have you had fun today? Learned something? Noticed somebody doing something right? Listened to somebody?

266. Be sure to tip the maid at least one dollar per night in the hotel/motel.

267. Even if it takes a course in creative writing, include on your expense account what you spend while out-of-town, even the movie and popcorn.

268. Don't follow all the instructions. Do something your own way. Become authentic and strive for your freedom.

269. Mail back to the hotel the keys you forgot to leave at the desk.

270. Tip more coming into the hotel than leaving and never, never carry your own bags.

271. Invite people to have breakfast with you (if they want to) and be ready to leave at the time they set.

272. Tip more than 15 or 20 percent if you keep a waiter/waitress' table longer than usual for business discussions.

273. Buy yourself an electric pot for boiling water and make your own coffee in the a.m. and tea in the p.m. while on the road. It's convenient in the morning and good for the soul in the afternoon. Besides, it saves you and/or the company a lot of money for room service.

274. Occasionally, stay in and do some work and have room service for dinner or supper. They must have a flower on your tray!

275. Go to bed early while out-of-town and rest. The weekend is for your wife or husband and family. Then, have a ball!

276. If you are still opening doors for your mother and wife, open doors for the women you work with. If you're not, you should.

277. Be generous with kindness, smiles and attention to everyone at all times.

278. Have a bird feeder.

279. Work in the yard. Helping a plant grow requires many of the same principles as helping yourself and others grow.

280. Decide what you really want to do and be persistent. "Hang in there."

281. To help decide what you really want to do, figure out your strengths, the skills that you enjoy using, determine where you would most want to do your dream, who you would most want to do it with, and then go for it. Read *What Color is Your Parachute.*

282. Learn to go from A to B to C. It's very rare for anyone to jump from A to Z.

283. Building a dream is so much more fun and rewarding than just having a dream.

284. But then I would rather have a dream and do nothing about it than not have a dream at all.

285. Find someone you admire, learn his or her beliefs and copy them. This will add to your strengths.

286. Learn more than necessary.

287. Reward failure.

288. Remember that you have everything you need. Maybe not what you want, but what you need is already yours.

289. You are already perfect; you don't need any more courses, seminars, books, or whatever to make you happy and have inner peace. Read *A Course in Miracles.*

290. "The key to happiness is making the decision to be happy."

291. We control how we respond to every stimulus and a lot of times it's just best not to respond.

292. It's the little things that get in the way of our doing a better job. Ignore the ones you can ignore, (you can learn this) put some others off until they just go away, prioritize the others and do them at the time you are the least productive.

293. Take your foot off first base. What's the worst that can happen? Go for it.

294. Plan for the best and have contingency plans for the worst.

295. Teach the culture of your company to all employees. Learn with them what the culture is. How would people describe what it's like to work with your company and your work group?

296. Are you a left-brained person or right-brained? Learn to use both. Be aware of where other people are coming from.

297. Remember, I'm Okay, You're Okay. Stay out of your critical parent, stay in your adult and develop a larger child. Read about Transactional Analysis to learn where you and others are coming from.

298. Being a good listener is also being aware of the other person's mind-set and not trying to change it.

299. Develop your curiosity and encourage the people you work with to keep asking "why."

300. Don't think or say that we are going to do it this way because we always have.

301. Don't say or think "If it's not broken, don't fix it." Keep looking for ways to improve it.

302. Quit focusing on measurements. Look for ideas from the people who are doing the job.

303.   Encourage and support the ideas and results that will be win-win for everybody.

304.   Look everywhere for ideas that can be developed into strategies. Read and share *Bottom-Up Marketing* and other books by the same authors.

305.
```
S   E   R   V   E
U   N   E   I   A
P   C   S   C   C
P   O   U   T   H
O   U   L   O   O
R   R   T   R   F
T   A   S   I   U
    G       O   S
    E       U
            S
```

306.   Implement your company plans but assume the responsibility for adding to and/or improving them with strategies developed "from the bottom" by your work group.

307.   Communicate new ideas and strategies to your home office, boss, and peers.

308.   One of our greatest strengths is our ability to change our thoughts.

309.   Leave your judgement somewhere else. Not at home. You can and they can when they are doing a good job.

310.   Learn how to get in there and help, but don't do the job for them. Give them your best.

311.   The energy you give out is the energy you will get back. Keep it positive and enthusiastic.

312.   Practice your "A's" - Appreciate, Accept, Adjust, Admire the people you depend on.

313.   Forgiveness is the way to love and love is the way to success, joy, and wisdom. Read *A Course in Miracles.*

314.   There are two emotions, fear and love. We are coming from one or the other.

315.   Any attack is coming from fear and is a request for love.

316.   We know when we are coming from love and so does the other person.

317.   Go with the flow, relax, quit fighting and working so hard and you will be surprised at the results.

318.   Take good care of yourself and others who are bringing in the results.

319.   Just say "no" to anything that compromises your values and principles.

320.   Always be willing to meet someone halfway.

321.   If you are not sure about a decision you are going to make, ask yourself:

        Is it against company policy or the law?

        Is it in balance? (Not 90% for you and 10% for the other guy.)

        Would you like to see your decision or action published in your local newspaper?

        Read: *Ethical Management* by Blanchard & Peale.

322.   Our power lies in the clarity of our vision and getting others to share it.

323.   The best investments you can make are in your career and a savings program.

324. Return all books that you borrow and don't give a book to someone until you have read it.

325. Don't follow all the rules, regulations, and directions. Become authentic.

326. Attend a noncompany sponsored business/management seminar at least once a year. Be willing to pay the cost yourself.

327. Spend some time with successful business people you know. Learn and share thoughts with them.

328. Buffer most of the stress, pressure, and negative thoughts from the people you work with.

329. Get to know the career placement and counseling people in at least a couple of universities and colleges for recruiting and on-campus interviewing.

330. Be willing to hire young people right out of college. Give them the positive experience that most people are looking for. Who gave you your chance?

331. Hire people with character who know some of their values and have a vision that is in harmony with the job. Be sure you like and enjoy being with them.

332. Implement a quality improvement program:

    Commit to continuing improvement

    Provide resources and wherewithal needed

    Develop teamwork

    Focus on processes/systems

    Satisfy customers

333. Learn to go an inch wide and a mile deep rather than a mile wide and an inch deep. (Read Deming's work and M. Walton's book on implementing the principles of Deming.)

334. We learn more from our peers than we do from managers and supervisors.

335. We can all learn from one another.

336. Most managers are overmanaging and underleading.

337. If you are getting a lot of obedience and "saluting," then you are not being as effective as you could be.

338. One of our purposes in life is to bring out the best within ourselves and others.

339. Develop patience.

340. We are all given a part of the universe to transform and improve. Ourselves.

341. Don't stay on the phone and in the office too much. A manager's place is out with the people he/she works with and with the customers.

342. We learn best from our mistakes and failures. Create a wide range of error for everybody.

343. An environment in which people will come to you with their needs will be productive and enjoyable.

344. Look for opportunities to compliment people.

345. Utilize love, not fear.

346. Create win-win, not win-lose situations.

347. Keep everybody well informed and beware of speculating with them.

348. Don't perform personal errands while working with people. This is their time.

349. We can become so preoccupied with things that are not important that we lose our connection with the things that are.

350. Speak the truth. Don't promise more than you can deliver. Keep your commitments.

351. Pay attention to the new people in your company and get to know them.

352. Sometimes it's best to reward people before they complete a task or achieve what you both want.

353. If you feel that people you work with need advice on personal matters, give it to them.

354. Hang out with people you enjoy and respect for doing a good job. Take the initiative to share with them.

355. Add your own ideas and suggestions to these and pass them on to someone else.

356. You can become an expert on something if you write about it. Figure out what you would most like to become really good at and keep a journal or write an article or book on the subject.

357. Get involved with your community, but only after your family and career are well tended to.

358. Money is very important, but work for your dreams, beliefs, values, and what you enjoy.

359. Remember that giving is the same as receiving.

360. Be willing to lose and fail, but share the insights, suggestions, and feedback that you honestly feel would contribute to your company.

361. Don't be fooled by your impressions. We can learn from everybody if we will just open up to them and remember that we are all joined together.

362. What you see in other people is what you will see in yourself.

363. You will see what you believe.

364. Build a tradition.

365. You will keep moving in your present direction. If you like it, speed it up. If you don't, change it.

366. Nothing is really yours until you give it away.

367. We will all, every one of us, check out with what we come in with. Enjoy the short time we are here.

368. Take good care of your mind, body, and spirit.

369. We will eventually lose our good health, but we never have to lose a good attitude.

370. We are so very much more than just our bodies. What are we attending to most?

371. Look for opportunities to help everyone feel proud of themselves, their job, and their company.

372. Make sure the people you work with realize that you are dependent on them for their success and yours.

373. Recognize and utilize all your resources. If you don't have what you need, invent it. Then share it. It's our responsibility to help make our company a better place to be.

374. If your company will not shift the paradigm, try tilting it yourself.

375. Sometimes the "nice guy" approach just does not work, but don't attack, just hang in there.

376. Love those that you care about...and who shouldn't you care about?

377. If customers buy for emotional needs or wants...and they do...then aren't we all working for emotional and spiritual reasons before the money? How about in addition to the money? How about after the money? Anyway, let's use a lot of other "things" besides money to help motivate ourselves and others.

378. Can you name at least six other motivational levers besides money? Yes or no? Let's read a good book on motivation. We don't motivate others, but we can make it easier for them to motivate themselves. And of course, we can also make it a hell of a lot harder! The choice is ours.

379. Act a certain way and that's the way you will become. (Norman Vincent Peale) In that case, let's choose to be happy. The decision starts the process.

380. If we are emotionally secure enough, we will not have to find fault with our predecessors and people we work with. Hey! We might not even have to reorganize or realign things to show we are the boss and the fellow before us was a bum.

381. The chances are you will work with some people who complicate the job, who keep the job simple, who have high standards, who have low standards, who are all different. This is just one reason why teamwork is the answer.

382.   Teach salespeople to call on customers in such a way that the customers are happy, enjoy the call, and get something worthwhile out of it. Then do the same for the people you work with. After all, they are your best customers.

383.   Ask your boss to send letters of congratulations to the people you work with in recognition of special achievements or progress they have made. Schedule a time for sending notes of congratulations and thanks.

384.   One of the best ways to solve problems is to anticipate them. What problems or opportunities will we have in six months, one year, or three years?

385.   We are not in the business of changing the people we work with. We are in the business of helping them grow.

386.   We are in the business of changing our customers, but only when they will be satisfied with the product or service we are selling.

387.   There are three sides to every story: yours, mine, and the truth.

388.   Remember, the sale is not completed until the customer is satisfied.

389.   "Seek to understand before being understood." (Steven Covey, *The Seven Habits of Highly Effective People*)

390.   You see what you believe and you believe what you value. Value the people on your team and the work they do.

391.   Demonstrate trust in the people you work with. Why not in all people?

392.   Look for opportunities to forgive others and yourself.

393. "What you give to others you are giving to yourself." *(A Course in Miracles)*

394. Being a successful manager depends on finding the right people and being the right person.

395. High expectations for yourself and others is a great motivator for personal development and achievement.

396. If you have to make a choice between personal development and achievement, go with personal development, but reward achievement.

397. Accept failure, disappointments, and problems as part of the job. They offer learning possibilities. Look for opportunities. They are so much more fun and motivating for others.

398. Try to operate within budgets and give budgets to your team members. This helps them to make decisions rather than you.

399. Believe people until proven otherwise. Remember: one time to learn, two times for action, and three times for decision.

400. Read *Life Is Not Fair But God is Good* by Robert Schuller.

401. Fair is at the fairgrounds in October.

402. If you become an expert in organization and time management, don't expect everybody else to. It goes against the nature of some people, but expect an acceptable amount from them.

403. In your office, do the tasks you like the least first so you will not let things build up and cause stress and frustration.

404. Judge your performance by results, quality and enjoyment.

405. We will do the things we are interested in when it's convenient, but for the things that we are committed to, we will only accept results.

406. Learn to enjoy music and flowers and being in the right place at the right time for creativity.

407 Learn to relax. Laugh at yourself. Not everything is so serious.

408. Look for opportunities to compliment people and when complimented, a simple "Thank You" is appropriate and sufficient.

409. When rooming with someone, always clean up the bathroom after yourself.

410. If you have business guests in your hotel room, always tidy up, make the bed, and clean up the bathroom.

411. Never go directly to someone's hotel room without calling first.

412. When tempted to criticize anybody, shut down your judgment, change the subject and move on. Watch out for the excuse of "constructive criticism." It's all the same. If you must criticize, criticize only the behavior, never the person, and only in private.

413. Love and forgiveness are the most powerful and under-utilized actions in management.

414. Most of us have been overmanaged with finger-pointing, criticism, faultfinding, and "do it this way," but it's our responsibility to respond with forgiveness and love.

415. Hang in there with an unbearable boss. "This too will change," and you will learn from the situation. Try to be helpful to him/her and do your job well.

416. Take the Dale Carnegie public speaking course and read his books. Even if you feel you don't have time, it's one evening a week for 14 weeks.

417. The question is not how to manage your time but how to manage your life. Everybody has the same amount of time but not the same values, purposes, goals, and priorities. Do you have yours written down?

418. Timing is so important. Don't delay taking action if you have enough information. Don't wait for all of the information. By that time, the opportunity could be gone. Be proactive.

419. To complete the most passes you will have to throw the most often and have the most interceptions.

420. Don't tell people to trust you. If you have to tell them that, then they probably don't.

421. Learn to do some things you don't want to do at the time you don't want to do it. And learn to do some things you want to at the time others want you to.

422. We have all the security we need. We have everything we need to be happy except maybe the decision.

423. Live your life and perform your job as an original. Become authentic.

424. Love is a very powerful and scary word to some people, but learn to tell people you love them.

425. Be old-fashioned in making time for people by being friendly and courteous and waving to people.

426. Get a copying machine for your office so that you can share articles that you enjoy with others.

427. Have a bulletin board in your office for posting current events and favorite and inspirational quotes. Share them.

428. Teach the people you work with how to evaluate their performance and learn how to evaluate and communicate your performance to your boss.

429. Encourage others to be independent and then teach them how to become effective team players.

430. Let others be decisive. You are the teacher and manager.

431. The length of time you will enjoy your job as a manager is based on the relationships you have with your group.

432. Autonomy is a much better motivator than money.

433. Be committed to the people you work with and your company. You will get commitment in return.

434. You cannot demand respect and commitment. They are only returned after you have given them to others.

435. The things you can demand and get are usually not important to running your business. They are only "window dressings."

436. Recognize and show appreciation for small improvements, as they are the basis for continuing improvement. This is what quality is all about.

437. When undecided about whether to hire someone, don't.

438. Commit yourself to an affirmative action program. All groups have their share of high achievers and offer real opportunities for outstanding people to join your company. The diversity is very helpful.

439. Learn how to welcome change.

440. The most difficult part of problem-solving is identifying the real problem and focusing on what you can change.

441. The best mind to have is an open mind.

442. Bars can be a nice place to relax and talk business. You don't have to drink but tip as if you were.

443. If you just stop and pick up a piece of litter, you are doing something about our environment.

444. When working with someone, occasionally have lunch in a park.

445. Two of the most effective phrases in management are, "I don't know. What do you think?"

446. Learn to run an enjoyable and productive meeting with lots of involvement and contribution from everyone present. Start and stop on time.

447. Focus on the important things that can be controlled, but listen to others who want to talk about things that cannot be controlled.

448. Listen and learn from the people who want to complain about your products, services, and ways of doing business.

449. Help people who may have a procrastination problem. It can be overcome.

450. Communicate the priorities of your business often and help assure that everyone knows their individual priorities.

451. Encourage goal-setting priorities and visualization of the end results.

452. With a commitment to others, we will be successful in business, our lives, and in the world.

453. Every encounter with another person is an opportunity to teach love or fear. We have the opportunity to begin and the choice is ours.

454. In our constantly continuing improvement, we need to see our work not as it is but what it could be.

455. Our career as a manager is important, but only to the extent that we are committed to serving others and nurturing the spirit within each of us. We can become so focused on trivial things that we lose connection with the important ones.

456. No problem is too small for us to listen to, and none is too large for a team to solve.

457. Momentum and progress are so important because they will keep moving in the intended direction.

458. Our problem is looking at the problem and not making the decision to embrace it.

459. An increase in attending and affirming others will improve results.

460. What we see, believe, think or expect of others, we will find in ourselves. We will become what we chose to be to them.

461. We will learn what we choose to teach and demonstrate. In every situation, we can teach love or fear. If we choose fear, we will become frightened. If we choose love, we will become positive and creative.

462. Forgiveness is the path to extending love because it is the way we change our thoughts from fear to love. This keeps us from judging and finding fault with others and ourselves.

463. When we become angry, resentful, or hold grievances, it's because of our difficulty with forgiving. These become indicators of our progress towards extending love.

464. We don't need to police the people we depend on or shake our finger at them to change. All we will do is make them defensive and less open to growth.

465. We all want to improve and will correct our weaknesses in a safe atmosphere of compassion, support and encouragement.

466. Whenever we attack someone, we are attacking ourselves.

467. If we become defensive because we are treated with harsh judgment, pressure, or attack, that defensiveness is a form of attack and no one can win. We should remain nonreactive or respond with love. We can't afford to settle for a lose-win or win-lose situation.

468. All casual encounters—with people in the grocery store, filling station, restaurants, etc.—can be seen as opportunities to practice compassion.

469. We will not be able to have a real teaching-learning relationship with everyone, but we will have some relationships that offer unlimited learning opportunities. Often, however, the people we can learn the most from are the ones who are not meeting our expectations and reflect back to us our own inability to care.

470. The form of our relationship will be different with everyone, but we are seeking the same content of care, trust, and mutual respect in all of our relationships.

471. The forms of our relationship will be dynamic and changing but can be recognized as teacher, learner, partner, manager, or friend.

472. When we are angry with someone, we are really angry at ourselves for our difficulty with forgiving or our other choice of response.

473. We need to spend more time helping others to realize their value rather than questioning how valuable they are.

474. We can tell others how they are rated and ranked, but can we tell them how wonderful they are?

475. Real work can only occur in the presence of candor, honest communicating, acceptance and authenticity.

476. Our purpose is to become the best that is within us. Part of the process is looking at what our strengths and improvement needs are, but remembering that we already have enough talents and are where we should be on our developmental path.

477. We would express love instead of negativity, if we knew how, and we would know how if we believed our needs could be met with love.

478. Our minds are perfect but we let them become covered with problems, poor work habits, and fear. We need to remember that this will be temporary if we don't attack other people, realize that problems don't last, and look for the opportunities that are there.

479. We let our relationships suffer because we focus on what others do wrong, what they are not doing, and what they need to learn. We need to look to ourselves, our perceptions, thoughts, and behavior to learn how to positively affect our part of the partnership.

480. If we want to be a positive influence on the career and lives of other people, we must learn to have a positive effect on our own career and lives. The first thing is to believe in the power of love.

481. In working with people, remember that we decide what we want to see before we see it. We will believe more in ourselves through our desire to believe in others.

482. To help salespeople improve, accept them as they are. They will feel better about themselves and more receptive to suggestions for growth.

483. The difference between criticism and suggestion is the difference between trying to change salespeople and accepting them.

484. If there is a key to working with others, it's the energy that our behavior carries. Is it fear, threat, and attack, or is it caring, acceptance, and support?

485. If someone is making a real mistake, they need teaching, not attacking.

486. We should not just tell salespeople that some of what they are doing, saying, or thinking is "fine, but..." and then attack. People only listen to what comes after the "but." If we are authentic and come from a base of support and acceptance, we can share our suggestions and alternatives successfully.

487. When we work from a base of love, we receive love from others. When we don't, they don't.

488. The highest award we can receive for being a manager is the joy of being an excellent manager/leader.

489. Being totally committed to each person we work with requires a commitment to mutual benefit, understanding, and forgiveness.

490. If we are not sure we have reached an agreement that is a win-win, let's keep communicating until we do. As a manager, let's don't settle for an easy win-lose situation.

491. The best way to keep people from competing with each other is for a manager to have a total commitment to each person, to the group, and to the common goals.

492. Managers need to give up the need for so much control.

493. Learn to love what you do by going to work each day to serve the needs of others.

494. When things are not going so well, we need to hang in there and work things out, but there are times when we need to help the other person to decide to leave.

495. Service means giving the needs of others the same priority as our own.

496. We are not held back by what we did or didn't do in the past, but by what we are not doing in the present.

497. We can work on extending compassion rather than fear at any moment of the day by practicing it.

498. Personal growth is about becoming the person we have the potential to be. The question is not what did we do yesterday, but what did we learn and what are we doing with it today.

499. Differentiate between "Leading" and Managing" by focusing on behaviors of each.

500.   Everything in the universe is structured to grow. You can change without growing, but you cannot grow without changing.

501.   Things which matter most must never be at the mercy of things which matter least.

502.   Add your own rules, and pass them on!

9

PART NINE

ABOUT THE AUTHOR

The Discovery Process: From Sales to Management and Back Again

My first sales experience was selling for an auto parts company during summers and in the afternoons of my senior year in high school. Sales work appealed to me, and as soon as I graduated from college with a Bachelor of Arts degree, I jumped right into the field with my first full-time sales job.

I worked for six months learning the products and the territory, long enough for me—and the company—to know that I could be successful as a salesperson.

The top 10% of our sales force (ranked by dollar sales per territory) received the Top Ten Award. I won this award three times during the five years I was eligible.

I now had a track record of success, but I was also fortunate to work alongside other top salespeople in the highest-performing work group in the country, and I accomplished other things that were more important to me than top sales awards. I gained a deep and abiding respect for salespeople, and I grew to love my career.

After about five years, however, I began to grow restless, wondering if it was time to move on. Just in the nick of time, I was promoted to Field Sales Trainer and handled the new responsibilities easily. It was enjoyable working with so many different salespeople and seeing the different approaches and hearing the various opinions and thoughts on what it took to sell.

The greatest thing that I learned in this position was that you could work more effectively with salespeople when you do not rely on authority. The salespeople trusted me. I had been one of them in the same division, and I never violated that trust. If they wanted to discuss certain subjects with me rather than with the manager, those discussions stayed with me.

I ended up spending two-thirds of my work time with salespeople and only one third in my territory—just the opposite of what we were supposed to do. The manager and the salespeople decided whom I was to work with and for what reasons. Another lesson that I learned was that you could get so much more "real stuff" done when the salespeople wanted you to work with them.

Everything that I reported to the manager was done on paper, with a copy to the salespeople. I did not recount anything that was not in the report. Openness is a great asset and is required for maintaining a positive relationship.

My First Job in Management

I could have stayed much longer in the job of Field Sales Trainer because I enjoyed it and felt that I was of help to some salespeople, but I was soon promoted to the position of Division Sales Manager. We were a new division and I had the opportunity to hire two new salespeople—the first in February and the next in April. This turned out to be one of my first and most important steps in building a successful new work group. After you accept a management position, your next important business decision is whom you are going to be working with because you are tying your success to them. I hired 70 percent of the division salespeople in those early years and learned several important lessons: hire and surround yourself with good people, then develop a good relationship with the people you work with by being honest and credible. You are dependent upon them to bring in the sales and contribute to the group and company. It is important to have high standards and expectations both for yourself and for others.

At the end of my first year of management our division was ranked only 24th out of 28 divisions, but we were building a strong foundation. By the end of the next year, we had won the President's Award for the top division in our region. We repeated this award the following year, and the year after that, we won the President's Award for being the top division and having the top manager in the nation.

We pushed for accomplishment: we developed a history and tradition for sales success; we established high standards for performance and business ethics; we won every contest that our company had in those years. We supported the company programs while understanding that it was our responsibility to improve the programs, not just apply them blindly. (You can follow the plan-of-action word for word and end up back on the farm.) We learned to contribute to one another and to compete not only with competitors but with our own individual and group potential. Four of our salespeople became successful division managers, and two went on to the home office. And I moved on as well.

To the Home Office

Before long, I decided to apply for a job in the home office myself. The decision to move was not an easy one.

I started my new job in the home office as Director of Distribution Services, and I reported to a department head who reported directly to the National Sales Manager. Our department ensured the availability and distribution of our products to wholesalers, and large accounts. It was also our responsibility to maintain contacts and build relationships with the national associations that represented each class of our customers. We set up programs to help field management identify and contact key people among our distributors. Having top-level and grass-roots work in concert greatly enhanced our results. We improved our distribution and our price-setting.

I had the opportunity to work directly with people who were senior in their positions and with very bright young people who were just beginning their career advancement in the home office.

Was the move worth it? Absolutely. Would I do it again? Absolutely. Did I learn? Absolutely.

My experience in the support staff function gave me a larger perspective, bringing home the realization that we were there to serve customers, salespeople and the community. Perhaps most importantly, the job taught me the power of listening to our customers to help us improve the way we did business.

Before long, though, I realized that I missed sales, salespeople, and sales management. When you are in sales, you know that what you do is important. You see the direct results of your contribution to others and to the company. In support functions—such as my Director of Distribution Services position—it is harder to see whether you are making a difference. For me, it was important work, but it was not sales.

Regional Sales Manager

When a regional sales manager's position became available nine months later, I jumped at the opportunity to get back into sales and sales management. It was not the same restlessness that I had experienced in the past when I sought promotion.

And it was not the money. There was plenty of opportunity in my present job for the future, and the department was doing well. What was it, then, that excited me about getting back into sales and sales management? What is it that is exciting, challenging and rewarding about sales and sales management to the people who are in it?

I discovered that sales was "home" for me. It was where I was meant to be. It's roots and it's tradition: it's a way of life. It's what I respond to and where I want to be. Selling evokes feelings of family and respect for others. Is it a "calling?" I don't think so. Most of us are responding to a hunger to make a difference, to be where we are at our best and where our best is never enough. Sales is a field where you want to keep growing and keep creating.

My old boss, my own regional manager in days past, had come through for me again with his encouragement and recommendations on my behalf. I had never thought of him as my mentor, perhaps because I did not know the word then. I do know that I felt he was the "unofficial leader" of the regional managers. We knew each other well because I had worked with him as a peer and only later reported to him as my manager. I learned a lot from him about "hands-off management"—or letting others do their jobs without interference. Easy to say, but so hard to do!

In the months before officially taking over the job, I learned several surprising things about the region I was to manage. The sales department had completed a very thorough and expensive Opinion/Attitude Survey done by an outside consulting firm. Opinion/Attitude Surveys are very helpful at identifying morale or motivational problems, the needs of the salespeople, and problems due to different managerial styles. This exhaustive survey clearly showed that the region I was taking over was in last place in the company. It had, by far, the greatest number of problems, most of which were caused by management practices.

Those faulty management practices could be summed up as:
- too much stress and pressure
- unrealistic and overly demanding sales goals or quotas
- short-term thinking
- lack of positive environment

The results of the Opinion/Attitude Survey should have come as no surprise. Pressure and stress—along with unreasonable goals, short-term thinking, and a negative environment—will always adversely affect sales and productivity. It was quite predictable that this region or work group would also be last in overall sales and sales by product.

Some managers greatly damage sales and productivity because their insecurity causes them to interfere with the salespeople's role. We need to be confident enough to allow qualified salespeople to do their job. Obviously, I'm a salesperson's manager and not a manager's manager. I believe in the salespeople first and foremost. They are the backbone of the success of any company. When I started my new job, I realized that I must make a conscious decision about whose side I would be on—the salesperson's or management's. I was determined to side with both, but I knew that I had to have a "majority opinion." My majority was going to be with the salespeople.

My primary concern as a regional manager, with 11 field managers and 120 salespeople reporting to me, was the bottom-line business results. After sales and productivity, personal development was the next most important focus. Our emphasis was on:
- building a positive work environment
- performance
- personal development
- letting managers run their divisions
- staying off the back of the salespeople

When I worked in the field with salespeople, I don't recall ever giving negative reports back to the managers, and this attitude helped improve our working environment.

I had seen firsthand the positive influence of the senior vice-president on the middle managers, administrative staff and the sales force. His influence was due to the trust the sales force had in him as a person and as a top executive. People felt free to share ideas with him and really say what was on their minds. Because he never violated this trust, he was really in touch with what was going on in the field, in the sales department, and in the company.

This senior V.P. believed in passing decision-making down to the lowest level possible. The salespeople decided which product to work out of the five or six being promoted, and it was their call which customers to sell it to, based on their potential and needs. He wanted the salespeople to choose from the wide range available, which sales tools to use in their presentations.

He believed that salespeople made the best decisions because they knew their customer base and what the customers' needs were. His philosophy was to hold each level responsible for making decisions about which they had the most information. He expected this informed decision-making from everyone—salespeople on up to top management. Interestingly, our personnel turnover during this time was very high because of the unwillingness of people to change and assume responsibility, but the turnover helped us develop an outstanding sales force and marketing organization.

During this time, I learned to give support and anything else they required, within reason, to the salespeople and field managers to help them do their jobs. With full support, they assume more accountability and responsibility for producing results because you are essentially eliminating any excuses for their not achieving their goals or the goals of the company. It's as if you say to them, "Here is a job. Here is what we need to achieve. What do you need? What do you want? What is getting in the way? You are in charge. You make the decisions." This approach builds healthy pressure to get the job done while not forgetting good ethics, business practices, and customer guidelines. The increased accountability and responsibility were a boon for the ones who wanted it, and it imposed higher standards on those who did not.

Full Circle

Though I learned much as a regional sales manager, I knew I could not stay there forever. What had gotten to me? I was crazy about the job and really involved in my work. My wife, five children, and mother were totally dependent on me financially. I couldn't just quit a job with nothing else lined up. Was I going nuts? Was it that restlessness again?

It wasn't restlessness. It was the most important lesson I had learned in my career.

It took me several months to realize you have to have your priorities in order, and I didn't. Betty wanted to raise our children in the area of the country where we had grown up. Our oldest son was going to be in the ninth grade, and she never forgot the time she moved when she was in the eleventh grade. Betty didn't want the children to have to go through that. I discovered that Betty and the children came first with me. They were more important than my career.

I was 36 years old and felt that I could find a job in sales or sales management for another firm and could be settled in another career by the time I turned 40. As it turned out, I didn't have to make such a radical move. I learned that trust— even blind trust—can work for you. When I told my boss that I didn't feel right about participating in an upcoming Organizational Development Program because I knew that I wanted to relocate, this was trust. Some would say "blind trust." My boss asked me not to do anything for several weeks. There was a division manager who was not working out in another part of the country and another manager who wanted to relocate. Maybe things would work out for me to return to my part of the country as a division manager, if the regional manager approved me for the position.

That's just what happened, and in January, I headquartered in my hometown. I had come full circle: from division manager to a home office job and then back to my own hometown. I would not take anything for the experience. For over two years I had been a regional manager, working with other managers. Could I apply these lessons to my new position? Can you really go back home again? Would the same job be as challenging as it had before? Would I get restless again? I did not know the answers to these questions. But, Betty was happy and we were where we wanted to be. I was determined to do my best. I was determined to work hard, to prove myself again.

The transition wasn't easy. Perhaps because of insecurity, I started to push, wanting results too fast. I tried to change the people I was working with. With three states in the new division, the broad geography made building a team difficult. Personnel problems seemed to overwhelm me. Sales were not good and our two largest and most important products were not available for use in a statewide program. Business problems were coming at me left and right.

Beyond business concerns, I had to make the most difficult and stressful personal decisions of my life: admitting my mother first to a hospital, then to the nursing home where she died. Experience has taught me that it's very difficult to separate personal and family problems from business problems. If your focus is limited to someone's business problems, goals or improvement, you are lucky if you can help that person 10%. If you can help someone with personal and family problems, you may help his/her business performance 90%. I believe management can help by listening, understanding, caring, talking about options and resources. All too often, managers really do not know what is going on in the other person's life until enormous problems emerge.

No one in our company knew what was going on in my life during this time. I did not try to keep the situation from anyone, but neither did I make any effort to talk about it.

To make matters worse, I soon had problems with my own health. I was admitted to the hospital in shock from a bleeding ulcer. I stayed six weeks, nearly dying after two operations and an abdominal infection. But I not only recovered fully, I came back stronger and happier. Although it took time, I had renewal, resurgence and rebuilding. I will say only this: no person will grow in business or in life without growing personally. Growing personally requires more than gaining skills and knowledge. It also requires spiritual growth.

One of my biggest challenges after the hospital and recovery was that I couldn't stand wasting time in unresolved disagreements with my spouse. I insisted that Betty and I see someone who could help us understand one another better. Our few sessions were very helpful. I often laugh to myself when I hear businesspeople talk about understanding their customers' needs. Most of us don't even understand our own needs or those of our spouses. The counseling was not only helpful in itself, it showed me the value of using all available resources to help you grow and reach your personal, family, and business goals.

Toward a New Way of Managing

It was during this time that I learned the most basic lesson of all: Before you can change the way you and your company do business, you must first make the necessary personal changes that improve the way you relate to the individuals around you. I was finally ready to begin making changes to get my struggling sales division back on track. I began by asking the salespeople what they considered to be the fundamentals and basics that had led to our past success in sales and management. We came up with this list:

- awareness of resources
- utilizing our resources
- developing a vision
- credibility
- contributing to others
- confidence
- respect for others
- relationships
- energy
- training/development
- learning
- trust
- focus
- enjoyment
- hiring
- deciding
- high standards for performance and ethics
- responsibility/accountability
- goal setting
- perseverance
- long-term viewpoint
- positive environment
- sales results
- productivity
- willingness to change
- risk taking
- support
- diversity
- priorities
- teamwork

These were the critical 30 fundamentals or concepts that had contributed to our success. We would build upon them.

After reviewing what had helped in the past, I made another important decision—a conscious decision—to talk more about business with my wife. As a result, Betty has become a valuable sounding board to me over the years, and I often refer to her as my #1 consultant. I don't mean to imply that she handles my work or tasks—she wouldn't even if I wanted her to. Instead, she listens and asks questions that help me deal with a particular issue, decision, or problem.

With the salespeople doing 90% of the work, our new group earned the company's top award for sales—a success we would repeat nine out of the next ten years. It took almost a decade, but we solved the problem of our two major products not being available for use in a statewide program. We also changed the system to keep this kind of availability problem from recurring.

We broke new ground again when I hired the first woman sales representative in our region, someone who continues to this day to be a stellar performer. She, in turn, helped me recruit and hire the only coworker I'm going to mention by name in this book—Sherry Poole. This book is dedicated to Sherry, with whom I worked for seven years. She taught me to recognize and acknowledge care and compassion in the world of business. This was a great thing to discover.

Sure, I had learned about these things from my mother. She used to say, "You will catch more flies with honey than vinegar." I often told myself, "I'll win them over with kindness." These examples, though, centered not on what the other person wanted but rather on trying to get what I wanted. Dennis Waitley has said, "You will get what you need by giving others what they want" and "I like myself best when I'm with you." These are more than catchy phrases; they are factual. There are some people who bring out the very best in us. This is what Sherry did for me. Our relationship was that of colleagues and

friends, and though she resigned in 1984, she remains a positive influence on me and my career. Sherry has had more to do
with my completing this book than anyone else, sending me
books to read with the comment, "You could have written
this—why didn't you?" Her continued support reminds me
that you never know what you may do and say to people that
will help convince them that they can achieve something they
never would have thought possible.

Encouragement, kindness, giving, compassion, peace, joy,
non-judgmentalness, acceptance. Are these factors of success
in business? Yes, absolutely. Unfortunately, they are often left
out in the harsh reality of the bottom line. It's certainly true
that without the right numbers, we would not have either a
business or jobs, but that does not mean that we have to
exclude the positives listed above. Like teaching, nursing, social
work, and the nurturing vocations, business also opens new
potentials for us to see and experience caring. Discussing and
sharing proven methods of incorporating caring and compassion into productive management techniques on a daily basis
is the core of *The Q-Factor.*

Bibliography and Suggested Reading

Autry, James. *Love & Profits: The Art of Caring Leadership,* William Morrow & Co., 1991.

Barker, Joel Arthur. *Future Edge.* William Morrow & Co., 1992.

Blanchard, Kenneth, Ph. D. and Patricia Zigarmi, Ed. D., and Drea Zigarmi, Ed. D. *Leadership and the One Minute Manager.* William Morrow & Co., 1985.

Blanchard, Kenneth, Ph. D. and Spencer Johnson. *The One Minute Manager.* William Morrow & Co., 1982.

Bracey, Hyles. *Managing from the Heart.* Dell Publishing Co., 1993.

Brown, H. Jackson Jr. *Life's Little Instruction Book.* Rutledge Hill Press, 1991.

Carlson, Richard and Benjamin Shield. *Handbook for the Soul.* Little, Brown & Co, 1995.

Covey, Stephen R., and A. Roger Merrill and Rebecca R. Merrill. *First Things First.* Simon & Schuster, 1994.

Covey, Stephen R, *The 7 Habits of Highly Effective People.* Simon & Schuster, 1989.

Deming, W. Edwards, Ph. D. *Out of the Crisis.* Cambridge, MA & M.I.T., 1986.

Dow, Roger & Susan Cook, *Turned On: Eight Timeless Principles for Energizing your Customers,* Harper Collins, 1996.

Drucker, Peter F. *Innovation and Entrepreneurship.* Harper and Row, Publishers, 1985.

Dyer, Wayne W., Ph. D. *Your Erroneous Zones.* Harper Collins Publisher, 1991.

Foundation for Inner Peace. *A Course in Miracles.* Foundation for Inner Peace, 1975.

Gerson, Richard F., Ph. D. *Measuring Customer Satisfaction.* Crisp Publications, Inc., 1993.

Harmon, Frederick G. *The Executive Odyssey.* John Wiley & Sons, 1989.

Hill, Napoleon, *Think and Grow Rich.* Ballentine Books, 1960.

Jampolsky, M.D., Gerald G. *Teach Only Love.* Bantam Books, Inc., 1983.

Joiner Associates. *The Practical Guide to Quality.* Joiner Associates, 1993.

Joiner Associates. *The Team Handbook: How to Use Teams to Improve Quality.* Joiner Associates, 1994.

Joiner Associates. *Fundamentals of Fourth Generation Management.* Joiner Associates, 1995.

Katzenbach, Jon R., and Douglas K. Smith. *The Wisdom of Teams.* McKinsey & Co., 1993.

Mackay, Harvey. *Beware the Naked Man Who Offers You His Shirt.* Ballentine Books, 1990.

Mackay, Harvey. *Swim With the Sharks Without Being Eaten Alive.* William Morrow & Co, 1988.

Millgate, Irvine H. *Teacher/Manager Systems.* Six Lights, Cutler, Maine, 1990.

Naisbitt, John, and Patricia Aburdene. *Re-inventing the Corporation.* Warner Books, 1985.

Nash, Laura L. *Good Intentions Aside.* McGraw-Hill Companies, 1990.

Parker, Glenn M. *Cross Functional Teams.* Jossey-Bass, Inc., 1994.

Peck, M. Scott, M.D. *Further Along the Road Less Traveled.* Simon & Schuster, 1993.

Peck, M. Scott, M.D. *The Road Less Traveled.* Bantam Books, 1990.

Peters, Tom, and Robert H. Waterman, Jr. *In Search of Excellence.* Warner Books, Inc., 1988.

Peters, Tom. *The Pursuit of Wow!* Vintage Books, 1994.

Peters, Tom. *The Tom Peters Seminar.* Random House, Inc., 1988.

Ries, Al, and Jack Trout. *Bottom-Up Marketing.* McGraw-Hill Companies, 1989.

Ries, Al, and Jack Trout. *Marketing Warfare.* McGraw-Hill Companies, 1986.

Riley, Pat. *The Winner Within.* G.P. Putnam & Sons, 1993.

Schaffer, Robert H. *The Breakthrough Strategy.* Ballinger Publishing Co., 1988.

Schuller, Robert. *Success is Never Ending, Failure is Never Final.* Bantam Books, 1990.

Schuller, Robert. *Tough Times Never Last, Tough People Do.* Bantam Books, 1984.

Schwartz, David J., Ph. D. *The Magic of Getting What You Want.* William Morrow & Co., 1983.

Schwartz, David J., Ph. D. *The Magic of Thinking Big.* Simon & Schuster, 1987.

Strusberg, Peter A. *One-Day Business Planning and Every Day Follow-Up.* Chilton Co., 1988.

Walton, Mary. *The Deming Management Method.* Putnam Publishing, 1986.

Williamson, Marianne. *A Return to Love.* Harper Collins Publisher, 1992.

We hope that *The Q-Factor* has been helpful to you. We would like to hear from you with your additional Rules of the Road and factors for improving business. Any suggested prioritization of The Rules of the Road could also be beneficial.

Frank Munson has been giving lectures and conducting sessions based on this book and *The Process for Learning, Sharing and Selling.*

For further information, write or call:

Frank Munson and Associates
2130 Shady Lane
Columbia, SC 29206
(803) 782-9123
(803) 782-1931 Fax

Money-Back Guarantee

Take the time for introspection and practice the opportunities for improvement that you discover in *The Q-Factor* for at least 21 days. If you feel that the results aren't worth more than what you paid for *The Q-Factor*, return it with your sales receipt within 45 days of purchase to the address above and I will send you a full refund. I am that sure the *The Q-Factor* works!

– Frank M. Munson